revelation of Revelation

AN URGENT MESSAGE FOR THE CHURCH

VOLUME 2
THE SEVEN LETTERS OF REVELATION

Rev 1:1-3:22

The Naked Apostles
Phil and Colleen Livingston

Published by: The Naked Apostles

WAUCONDA, IL

Phil and Colleen Livingston/The Naked Apostles
304 Barrington Road
Wauconda, IL 60084
www.nakedapostles.org
email: info@nakedapostles.org

Ordering Information:
Quantity sales. Special discounts are available on quantity purchases by corporations, associations, and others. For details, contact via email or the address above.

revelation of Revelation, *An Urgent Message for the Church* Volume 2: The Seven Letters of Revelation/The Naked Apostles, Phil and Colleen Livingston. 2.2
ISBN-978-0-9960102-5-2

Table of Contents

Dedicated to the Church of Philadelphia

"You will say, Christ saith this, and the apostles say this; but what canst thou say? Art thou a child of Light and hast walked in the Light, and what thou speakest is it inwardly from God?"

George Fox

1624-1690

He who overcomes will inherit these things; and I will be his God and he will be My son.

— Revelation 21:7 New American Standard Bible

CHAPTER 1

The Jewish Numbering System

There are no numeric symbols in the Hebrew language. The letters of their alphabet have a numeric value. Each letter has a deep spiritual meaning and significance as well. In addition to that, the numeric values of each letter also have a deep spiritual meaning and significance.

There are some important things to understand about their counting system compared to ours. Knowing the differences will help us understand the Hebrew symbolic uses of numbers. Our modern math is from an Indian-Arabic numbering system. The Hebrews don't have a zero. Zero is a place holder in what is called a place holder system, like the numbering system we use. Our numbering system is called a base ten system.

Take a number like 287, base ten refers to the position, the 7 is in the one's place, the 8 is in the ten's place and the 2 is in the hundred's place. Each number is 10 times the value to the right of it, hence the term base ten. The numbers continue indefinitely in this pattern. The Hebrew numbering system is not a base system because it is not a positional system. To say a number like 287, you would have to write out 200, 80, and 7, all being shown as three different letters. The letter's position does not matter, they come out to the same value. Using the three Hebrew letters in a different order like 7, 200, and 80 comes out to the same value 287. In our numbering system, which is positional, 728 would have a completely different value than 287.

One other note is that having only 22 letters in their alphabet, they only have 22 numbers. Below is a chart showing the Hebrew letters and their numeric value:

Hebrew Numeric System

Figure 1

Sequence Order	Character	Hebrew Letter Name	Numerical Value
1	א	ALEF	1
2	ב	BET	2
3	ג	GIMEL	3
4	ד	DALET	4
5	ה	HE	5
6	ו	VAV	6
7	ז	ZAYIN	7
8	ח	HET	8
9	ט	TET	9
10	י	YOD	10
11	כ	KAF	20
12	ל	LAMED	30
13	מ	MEM	40
14	נ	NUN	50
15	ס	SAMEKH	60
16	ע	AYIN	70
17	פ	PE	80
18	צ	TSADI	90
19	ק	QOF	100
20	ר	RESH	200
21	ש	SHIN	300
22	ת	TAV	400

There are Hebrew symbols that are used to represent large quantities like 1,000 or 10,000, however, for the sake of this study we won't go into it, except to say that if you have a number that is not one of the 22 letters, then you have to use multiple letters to add until you get the quantity you are looking for. Like for example, to write 19 you would use the letters which represent 10 and 9.

There is an exception to this when it comes to the numbers 15 and 16. If the last two digits of a number are 15 or 16, they should be expressed not as YUD HE (10+5) and YUD VAV (10+6), but as TET VAV (9+6) and TET ZAYIN (9+7). This is done to avoid a close resemblance to the Tetragrammaton (four-letter name of God which the Hebrews think is too sacred to be pronounced) YUD HE VAV HE. Pointing this out is important to show how the spiritual significance and meaning of each letter and its numeric value is so important to the understanding of their meaning.

It is written in Jewish literature that God taught Abraham many things. However, until God taught Abraham the Hebrew language, he could not have full revelation and understanding of God's teachings. Each letter and its numeric value has so much spiritual meaning that to learn something of the spiritual using the Hebrew language, you can almost go on forever having infinite revelation about even the smallest morsel of knowledge.

In Revelation, there are four numbers used which will be very important to understand their Hebrew significance as well as the number seventy in Daniel. They are: four, seven, eight, ten, and seventy. Seven is not only the most used, but has the most significance when trying to interpret Revelation.

Four is used to describe the four living creatures in heaven; four horns of the golden altar; four natures of the beast, four corners of the earth, four angels which held back the four winds of the earth; and four angels who were bound at the great river Euphrates.

WEB Rev 7:1 After this, I saw four angels standing at the four corners of the earth, holding the four winds of the earth, so that no wind would blow on the earth, or on the sea, or on any tree.

Four

Then people will come from east and west, from north and south, and will eat in the kingdom of God. (Luke 13:29)

Four is the creation number and it has special significance to the earth. Four is symbolic of earthly completeness (*or comprehensiveness, or all inclusiveness*). On the fourth day, all materials for the earth were created. Four is the number of the great elements: earth, air, fire, and water. There are four regions or directions: north, south, east, and west. There are four seasons of the year: fall, winter, spring, and summer. There are four phases of the moon: first, half, full, and last. There are four divisions of the day: morning, noon, evening, and night. The Bible also has ten references to the four winds.

The number four indicates universality. This means that from one point to the next point, everything is included such as in the Scripture above. It is universal participation. All people will come from all four corners of the earth to enjoy the kingdom of God as is illustrated in the four gospels: Matthew, Mark, Luke and John.

Four in the Scriptures portrays universal observation, worship and adoration as in Revelation 4:6-8. "Around the throne, and on each side of the throne, are four living creatures, full of eyes in front and behind: the first living creature like a lion, the second living creature like an ox, the third living creature with a face like a human face, and the fourth living creature like a flying eagle."

Jesus appeared as the fourth man to save the three Hebrew boys (Daniel 3:25). He will do the same for you.[1]

The use of four in prophecy:

Amp Rev 7:1 AFTER THIS *I saw four angels stationed at the four corners of the earth,* **firmly holding back the four winds of the earth** *so that no wind should blow on the earth or sea or upon any tree.*

Amp Rev 7:2 Then I saw a second angel coming up from the east (the rising of the sun) and carrying the seal of the living God. And with a loud voice he called out to the four angels who had been given authority and power to injure earth and sea,

Amp Rev 7:3 Saying, Harm neither the earth nor the sea nor the trees, until we have sealed the bond servants of our God upon their foreheads.

The bond servants are the 144,000 starting with Abraham, which had need of being marked for protection before the four winds of destruction or the four angels of destruction were released on the earth. Who or what are the four winds?

The four winds of the earth are the judgment of God and are the winds of His destruction. They are the first four seals which describe the four horsemen of the apocalypse; the grey horse, the red horse, the black horse, and the pale horse. They were released soon after the flood when God decided to judge the world with fire, as a result of all the people of the earth making the beast, Nimrod, king over them in order to be independent of and rebellious towards God. However, we are told that this released judgment was held back so that the 144,000 could be marked and exempt from harm by these four winds of destruction which the earth would now be cursed with. They were exempt because God's plan of redemption, the Christ (the fifth seal), came through them, who are also known as the first fruits. There are four angles from God not allowing them to be released until the plan of God is protected.

Horses represent power. The horses the four angels of destruction ride are the power they have to achieve conquest and rule the world: to take peace from the earth and cause men to slay each other through war; enslave the nations; and finally enforce the former three powers with the fourth, death. Death on a scale the earth has never known aside from the flood; diseases, famine, natural disasters, and by animals/nature. Again, within the four horsemen, there are four ways nature—the very environment our lives are sustained by—has become a curse to man. Finally, this judgment of God, this curse of the world becoming hostile towards man allows an ongoing 25% or 1/4 of the lives of the human race to be prematurely taken by death through the four winds of destruction/the four horsemen.

The importance of using four as a number and to describe these curses on mankind is to give the reader a sense of complete comprehensiveness and inclusion. We all are touched by these curses and they are something pronounced on the whole world; no one is exempt.

Eight

Then Abraham circumcised his son Isaac when he was eight days old, as God had commanded him. (Genesis 21:4)

The number eight symbolizes resurrection and a new beginning. Noah's ark passed through the waters symbolizing death, but it was resurrected and rested on Mt. Ararat and eight people emerged to a new beginning.

Why did God command Jewish males to be circumcised on the eighth day? Why not on the first day or much later? Eight means "as above, so below." That's why Jewish male babies are circumcised on the eighth day to seal the covenant with God. "And when eight days were completed for the circumcision of the Child, His name was called Jesus, the name given by the angel before He was conceived in the womb" (Luke 2:21).

Other interesting things about the number eight: David was the eighth son of Jesse, while Solomon was the eighth son of David. The writers of the New Testament were eight in number: Matthew, Mark, Luke, John, Paul, James, Peter and Jude. Christ is the Resurrection and the Life. His birth place, Bethlehem, is mentioned exactly eight times in the New Testament. Jesus came that we might have a new beginning. Accept Him today and begin your life anew.[1]

Eight represents a new beginning or a new cycle. Seven means completion and perfection. When God created the world in seven days the eighth day began a new week. When Jesus was raised from death it was on Sunday, the first day of the new week. This signified a new beginning.

The number eight in Revelation:

NIV Rev 17:7 *Then the angel said to me: "Why are you astonished? I will explain to you the mystery of the woman and of the beast she rides, which has the seven heads and ten horns.*
NIV Rev 17:8 *The beast, which you saw, once was, now is not, and will come up out of the Abyss and go to his destruction. The inhabitants of the earth whose names have not been written in the book of life from the creation of the world will be astonished when they see the beast, because he once was, now is not, and yet will come.*
NIV Rev 17:9 *"This calls for a mind with wisdom. The seven heads are seven hills on which the woman sits.*

NIV Rev 17:10 *They are also seven kings. Five have fallen, one is, the other has not yet come; but when he does come, he must remain for a little while.*

NIV Rev 17:11 *The beast who once was, and now is not, **is an eighth king**. He belongs to the seven and is going to his destruction.*

NIV Rev 17:12 *"The ten horns you saw are ten kings who have not yet received a kingdom, but who for one hour will receive authority as kings along with the beast.*

NIV Rev 17:13 *They have one purpose and will give their power and authority to the beast.*

The eighth king: In Revelation, the beast is described as having seven heads and ten horns. One of the things the seven heads represent is seven kings. Then it tells us there is an eighth king. This seemingly is a real wrench in the works. There is almost too much to make sense of here. You have one beast with seven heads which are, among other things, seven kings. Then this same seven headed beast has ten horns which are also ten kings. Then we have an eighth king who is one of the seven. How does this make sense? Because if the eighth king is one of the seven, how then is he an eighth king? If he is one of the seven, then there would be only seven, not eight kings. Because of this problem most translations say the eighth king is "of" the seven. Where some say he is "one" of the seven; even though it doesn't make sense.

To sum up, these seven heads represent among other things seven empires/kingdoms, seven kings, seven hills (giving a geographical location, as we will see later). One of the heads/king/kingdom has ten more kings and there is an eighth king but at the same time, he is one of the other seven. Add to this, those seven empires had multiple kings. The Roman Empire alone, both east and west, had as many as 270 kings.

Getting back to this "eighth king," the proper translation is that he is "one" of the seven and we will see how this is true. Let us look at the verses which tell us about this eighth king and the significance of him being the eighth according to the Hebrew meaning of the number 8:

NIV Rev 17:8a *The beast, which you saw, once was, now is not, and will come up out of the Abyss and go to his destruction.*

An interesting fact to take note of is that we hear about this eighth king in verse 8. Verse 8 is telling us that the beast himself is a person who once lived *(once was)*, who is not alive at present when John was given this prophecy *(now is not),* and will rise up from among the dead, in the Abyss, and come back to life to rule *(and will come up out of the Abyss).* Nimrod the antichrist and founder of Babylon is the beast.

NIV Rev 17:8b The inhabitants of the earth whose names have not been written in the book of life from the creation of the world will be astonished when they see the beast, because he once was, now is not, and yet will come.

Verse 8 (above) continues on to say that every person who ever lived, alive and dead, since the creation of the world will be shocked when they see the beast come back from the dead, no longer disembodied. That is with the exception of the elect who know and understand Scriptures or already have their celestial bodies. They are not surprised by this development because God has told them in these very verses. It says again, that the reason for their astonishment is that this person, the beast, was a living person at one time, died (becoming a disembodied soul) and will come back to life clothed once again in a body to be among the living on the earth.

NIV Rev 17:10 They are also seven kings. Five have fallen, one is, the other has not yet come; but when he does come, he must remain for a little while.

These seven kings verse 10 (above) is speaking about are the seven shepherds of Babylon prophesied in Micah chapter 5. We are told that as of the time John received this prophecy five of those kings have lived and died *(Five have fallen).* The sixth is still alive and in power as the emperor of the Roman Empire *(one is).* Finally, the seventh will come, as of when John was given this prophecy *(the other has not yet come)* and when he does he <u>must </u>remain a little while *(but when he does come, he must remain for a little while).* That seventh shepherd/king is Pope Leo III and the succession of popes who rule his legacy as long as the Catholic Church remains a power. Indeed this kingdom has remained a while, since 800 AD when Leo revived the Roman Empire.

NAS REV 17:11 "The beast which was and is not, is himself also an eighth and is one of the seven, and he goes to destruction.

Verse 11 (above) continues on by informing us that the beast who was a person that lived in the past, died, and when he comes back to life will be the 8th king/shepherd of Babylon. Furthermore, for identification purposes, when he was alive in the past he was formerly one of the seven kings/shepherds. Obviously, he is one of the five who had already lived and died at the time John received this prophecy. In fact, he was the first king who established Babylon. Micah's prophecy agrees with this when it says:

*NIV Mic 5:5 ... When the Assyrian invades our land and marches through our fortresses, we will raise against him seven shepherds, even **eight leaders** of men.*
NIV Mic 5:6 They will rule the land of Assyria with the sword, the land of Nimrod with drawn sword.

From the beginning of God's plan and ordained destiny of judgment there was always going to be 8 kingdoms with 7 kings. Although there are only 7 kings ordained, the first of those 7 kings will return from the dead and claim the legacy of kingdoms that he himself established and set into motion so many thousands of years ago.

NIV Rev 17:12 "The ten horns you saw are ten kings who have not yet received a kingdom, but who for one hour will receive authority as kings along with the beast.
NIV Rev 17:13 They have one purpose and will give their power and authority to the beast.

When Nimrod rises from the dead and takes his kingdom by destroying the 7th kingdom, the Christian Church, he will divide the globe into 10 different districts giving 10 different leaders/kings charge of them. As we are told in the verses above, the beast will rule them all. Those 10 kingdoms or districts will use their power to serve the beast.

It reads, "who for one hour will receive authority as kings along with the beast". "One hour" is a term meant to describe a single cycle of time. In this case, that cycle of time is a week of years, meaning a 7 year period. It was mentioned previously when it came to the 7th seal that there was silence in heaven for about a half an hour. That was not only referring to the same length of a cycle of time, a week of years, but it was referencing the very same week of years which are talked about in this place. In other words, for the first half an hour, or first 3-1/2 years, of the 7 years, the beast and his 10 kings will rule of the entire globe. Heaven will be silent, or inactive, it will not intervene and there will be a global desolation of God's presence and activity in the world. It is only under the circumstances of a global desolation of God's presence that the beast, Nimrod, could perpetrate the most heinous evil ever visited upon the earth, the great tribulation. However, for the second half of his hour of power, or the last 3-1/2 years of his rule, the desolation of God's presence will end and He will preserve the lives of the balance of the elect. At the same time, He will punish the global kingdom of Nimrod, the beast. God will do so using heavenly or spiritual creatures.

Getting back to the usage of the number 8 in this prophecy, 8 means; new beginning. Nimrod, who was the first king of the world and had died, will have a new beginning by being granted life for the second time. Additionally, according to the same prophecy he will have a new beginning, or second time at being king of the world. However, this time it will be a true and complete fulfillment of what God ordained and spoke into existence. It will be no longer a partial and restrained rule, but total domination of the entire globe without any restraint of that power by God, His Son Jesus, the Holy Spirit or the four angels at the four corners of the earth holding him and his power back from complete rule.

When that happens, it will be because the whole world wants it that way, and has called him back from the Abyss in Hades through the power of the false prophet. This is the true reality of what will be in the "new age." The world believes this is an age for a thousand years, however, in reality it is short lived. The Bible has already told us the true nature of that time when supernatural or spiritual beings will manifest and interact with the natural. The appearance of the beast is just the beginning of what will follow. This is the age that spiritualists, practitioners of metaphysics, and the "new agers" have been calling down, advancing, and referring to as the "new age". They all are blissfully ignorant of what they are truly calling down upon their own heads.

Again, that "new age" to come is nothing more than a new beginning of what was loosed on the earth during pre-flood times and was put to an end by God's judgment. The boundaries between the natural and the supernatural had been dismantled and abominations of nature walked the earth. This was the very reason God judged the world with the flood, and destroyed these influences in the world, keeping them confined in the Abyss region of Hades.

Ever since Nimrod went into defiance against God a couple of generations after the flood, he spent his life searching for and seeking after reviving the pre-flood conditions and ways as a means to empower himself. He did so with no fear of any further consequences from God. In fact, he boasted and proclaimed he would protect the people of the earth against Yahweh so that they could do as they pleased. It was then in their defiance towards God that the world made Nimrod king over themselves. Since then, the overwhelming majority of the world through its religious practices, mythologies, philosophies, and spiritual endeavors have been calling down what Nimrod started.

God is judging and condemning humanity by giving us exactly what we have been asking for, for thousands of years. As this study advances, it will show through the book of Revelation exactly what that time of the "new age" will look like. It will show exactly what the supernatural will visit upon the earth when the old and dead pre-flood ways are given that new beginning the number 8 represents.

The days of the new age or the new beginning for the beast are numbered to only seven years. There are so many promises of what the "new agers" are looking forward to in that day. Abilities which are supernatural; to live forever, to transcend sickness, to be able to teleport and to communicate spirit to spirit without words, to interact with supernatural beings or aliens from different planets. However, the Bible (below) tells us what the new age will be like:

WEB Rev 16:12 *The sixth poured out his bowl on the great river, the Euphrates. Its water was dried up, that the way might be prepared for the kings that come from the sunrise (out of the east).* [13] *I saw coming out of the mouth of the dragon, and out of the mouth of the beast, and out of the mouth of the false prophet, three unclean spirits, something like frogs;* [14] *for they are spirits of demons, performing signs; which go out to the kings of the whole inhabited earth, to gather them together for the war of that great day of God, the Almighty.*

WEB Rev 8:13 I saw, and I heard an eagle, flying in mid heaven, saying with a loud voice, "Woe! Woe! Woe for those who dwell on the earth, because of the other voices of the trumpets of the three angels, who are yet to sound!"

WEB Rev 9:1 The fifth angel sounded, and I saw a star from the sky which had fallen to the earth. The key to the pit of the abyss was given to him. ² He opened the pit of the abyss, and smoke went up out of the pit, like the smoke from a burning furnace. The sun and the air were darkened because of the smoke from the pit.

The star which falls is the Devil himself being thrown out of the spiritual realm down to earth. This event is also described in chapter 12:

NIV Rev 12:7 And there was war in heaven. Michael and his angels fought against the dragon, and the dragon and his angels fought back.

NIV Rev 12:8 But he was not strong enough, and they lost their place in heaven.

NIV Rev 12:9 The great dragon was hurled down—that ancient serpent called the devil, or Satan, who leads the whole world astray. He was hurled to the earth, and his angels with him.

NIV Rev 12:10 Then I heard a loud voice in heaven say: "Now have come the salvation and the power and the kingdom of our God, and the authority of his Christ. For the accuser of our brothers, who accuses them before our God day and night, has been hurled down.

NIV Rev 12:11 They overcame him by the blood of the Lamb and by the word of their testimony; they did not love their lives so much as to shrink from death (during the great tribulation).

NIV Rev 12:12 Therefore rejoice, you heavens and you who dwell in them! But woe to the earth and the sea, because the devil has gone down to you! He is filled with fury, because he knows that his time is short."

This is not a figurative, but a literal event and is supported by other Scriptures. At that time the earth will not just suffer from the invisible spirit force of the Devil, but we will see his form and suffer his power and wrath. The earth will be visited by whom the Roman and Greek mythologies believe is the god Zeus/Jupiter, the king of the gods. According to what the above verses are saying with him comes his host of fallen angels. In addition, he is given the ability to release all the supernatural beings who are confined to the Abyss so they too may manifest on the earth.

This is incredible! The Abyss is a place in Hades. Hades is the realm of the dead where the disembodied souls of humans who have died are confined. The Abyss is a place within Hades, and is the place of confinement meant for all the fallen angels who bred with natural women and other natural creatures, as well as the half-natural, half-celestial creatures they produced; including the giants or Nephilim which once dominated the earth. The Abyss is like the high security place in prisons separate from the general population. The Abyss is a special place of confinement and torment which exceeds that of hell in Hades.

The angels who mixed there celestial DNA with natural creatures are the gods of mythologies around the world. Their spawn of half-celestial, half-natural humans were giants and are the demigods of the mythologies in the world. When God had enough of the abominations in the earth, He judged the world with a flood. The dead, the disembodied souls who died in the flood, were confined in Hades. The angels (the gods of mythologies) and the giants (the demigods they spawned) were confined in a special place within Hades called, the Abyss, or the bottomless pit, in order that they could not interfere with the affairs of men, or dominate them or procreate with them.

Nimrod's disembodied soul we learn in the Bible, is now confined in this place reserved for the worst of the worst—the Abyss. He is not held in the hellish place in Hades like the rest of the disembodied souls of evil men awaiting the last day of judgment. That fact alone speaks much of his infamy, and supports the fact that he was called a giant or demigod by antiquity. Since the flood humanity has been set free from the scourge and horrors of the pre-flood world. Since Nimrod began his pursuits, power hungry people who desire supernatural powers have done whatever possible to recreate and tap into those powers which the earth suffered from and facilitated the flood. They will finally get what they want.

When the Devil is cast down to the earth and is manifest, everything which the Abyss kept humanity safe from, will be released from confinement and allowed to interface with the natural world again. Below is a description of what that will look like and what the new beginning of the "new age" will bring:

WEB Rev 9:3 Then out of the smoke came locusts on the earth, and power was given to them, as the scorpions of the earth have power. 4 They were told that they should not hurt the grass of the earth, neither any green thing, neither any tree, but only those people who don't have God's seal on their foreheads. ⁵ They were given power not to kill them, but to torment them for five months. Their torment was like the torment of a scorpion, when it strikes a person. ⁶ In those days people will seek death, and will in no way find it. They will desire to die, and death will flee from them. ⁷ The shapes of the locusts were like horses prepared for war. On their heads were something like golden crowns, and their faces were like people's faces. ⁸ They had hair like women's hair, and their teeth were like those of lions. ⁹ They had breastplates, like breastplates of iron. The sound of their wings was like the sound of chariots, or of many horses rushing to war. ¹⁰ They have tails like those of scorpions, and stings. In their tails they have power to harm men for five months. ¹¹ They have over them as king the angel of the abyss. His name in Hebrew is "Abaddon", but in Greek, he has the name "Apollyon".¹² The first woe is past. Behold, there are still two woes coming after this. ¹³ The sixth angel sounded. I heard a voice from the horns of the golden altar which is before God, ¹⁴ saying to the sixth angel who had the trumpet, "Free the four angels who are bound at the great river Euphrates!" ¹⁵ The four angels were freed who had been prepared for that hour and day and month and year, so that they might kill one third of mankind. ¹⁶ The number of the armies of the horsemen was two hundred million. I heard the number of them. ¹⁷ Thus I saw the horses in the vision, and those who sat on them, having breastplates of fiery red, hyacinth blue, and sulfur yellow; and the horses' heads resembled lions' heads. Out of their mouths proceed fire, smoke, and sulfur. ¹⁸ By these three plagues were one third of mankind killed: by the fire, the smoke, and the sulfur, which proceeded out of their mouths. ¹⁹ For the power of the horses is in their mouths, and in their tails. For their tails are like serpents, and have heads, and with them they harm. ²⁰ The rest of mankind, who were not killed with these plagues, didn't repent of the works of their hands, that they wouldn't worship demons, and the idols of gold, and of silver, and of brass, and of stone, and of wood; which can't see, hear, or walk. ²¹ They didn't repent of their murders (of the elect during the great tribulation), *their sorceries, their sexual immorality, or their thefts.*

The above is what is in store for all those "new agers" who await the coming "new age", "the age of Aquarius." They think that it is an age of supernatural powers and being able to overcome illness and death through science and the supernatural. A time of total "freedom" and "peace." In their independence from God, self-reliance, and greed for spiritual power they are deceived into thinking man can achieve greatness and perfection in his own strength and intelligence.

In reality, however, their quest causes an opening of hell/the Abyss. As a result of the boundaries between the natural and the supernatural being once again removed, the confined supernatural beings are released into the world. It is a false freedom which in reality is merely a complete independence from God and an absence of His influence in human affairs—a time of no restraints.

WEB Mt 24:37 *"As the days of Noah were, so will be the coming of the Son of Man. 38 For as in those days which were before the flood they were eating and drinking, marrying and giving in marriage, until the day that Noah entered into the ship, 39 and they didn't know until the flood came, and took them all away, so will be the coming of the Son of Man..."*

The use of the number 8, when it comes to the 8th kingdom of the beast giving the people of the world what they desire, indeed results in a new beginning. However, the new beginning or new age they seek after will be much more than they bargained for.

Ten

And He wrote on the tablets the words of the covenant, the Ten Commandments. (Exodus 34:28)

There are four biblical numbers in the Bible that denote completion or perfection. Three, seven, ten, and twelve all mean completion and perfection. While each number represents completion or perfection, it is a different type of completion or perfection. Three means "divine perfection." Seven means "spiritual perfection." Twelve means "governmental perfection." That's why there are twelve people on a jury. Ten is the number of perfection or completion of God's "divine order." It is the only one of the perfect biblical numbers in which humans have a part. We cannot be part of the three, seven, or twelve. We are definitely part of the ten since it is the number of completion based on God's order AND human responsibility. The number ten is built into our very anatomy. For instance, we have ten fingers to do God's work and ten toes to walk upright before God. *(but not just 10 fingers and 10 toes but 5 and 5 fingers and 5 and 5 toes, signifying the completion of both God's order on the one hand and human responsibility on the other)*

Why only Ten Commandments in the Old Testament? Why not fifteen or twenty? The Ten Commandments contain all that is necessary, and no more than is necessary, both as to their number and their order. They are examples of God's order and man's responsibility. The first five concern our relationship with God. The last five concern our relationships with other humans. The number ten is the start of a whole new order of numbers and the completion of the single digit numbers that come before it. Our responsibility in stewardship is to give God ten percent of our first fruits because the tithes represent the whole of what is due from man to God' based on His claim on the whole.

We cannot aspire to divine perfection on our own. We cannot aspire to spiritual perfection on our own. We cannot attain governmental perfection without God. We can honor God's covenant according to His order and our responsibility.[1]

Ten is used in Revelation (and in Daniel) in these following verses:

WEB Rev 2:10 *Don't be afraid of the things which you are about to suffer. Behold, the devil is about to throw some of you into prison, that you may be tested; and you will have oppression for ten days. Be faithful to death, and I will give you the crown of life.*

WEB Rev 13:1 *I saw a beast coming up out of the sea, having ten horns and seven heads. On his horns were ten crowns, and on his heads, blasphemous names.*

WEB Da 7:7 *After this I saw in the night visions, and, behold, a fourth animal, awesome and powerful, and strong exceedingly; and it had great iron teeth; it devoured and broke in pieces, and stamped the residue with its feet: and it was diverse from all the animals that were before it; and it had ten horns.*

The meaning of 10, likewise, encapsulate a fullness of time or completeness. The number 10 in Hebrew message: If we are humble God's hand can direct our lives so that we can return and live with Him again. Thus the Ten Commandments to follow. Thus the 10 days of testing by the Devil, can humble us so the Lord can save us.

Ten signifies: God's order, testimony, law, responsibility. To say there were 10 of them, is akin to saying in our day, there were a million of them, or, to the tenth (umpteenth) power.

Completeness of order marking the entire round of anything is, therefore, the ever-present significance of the number ten. It implies that nothing is wanting; that the number and order are perfect; that the whole cycle is complete, on both sides.

So when the Lord says in Revelation you will suffer for 10 days, He is at the same time saying there will be no useless suffering you must go through. As soon as what is required is complete, I will put an end to it! I assure you by the use of the number 10, I will not put you through something that will serve only to pain you!

Seventy

Of particular interest, however, is the number 70, since it occurs frequently within Scripture and Jewish tradition. In Scripture we read that 70 souls went into Egypt, 70 elders of Israel saw the God of Israel on Mt. Sinai, 70 sacrifices made for the nations (during the festival of Sukkot), and Israel was subject to 70 years of exile in Babylon. In Jewish tradition, there are 70 members of the Sanhedrin, 70 words of Kaddish, 70 " faces of Torah" 70 Names of God, and 70 birth pangs until the coming of the Mashiach. (also 70 scribes translated the Septuagint from Hebrew to Greek)[2]

70 **ayin** signifies perfect spiritual order carried out with significant spiritual power; nations; human committees; judgment of God's people; God administrating the world; eye; insight; Moses appointed 70 elders; Sanhedrin; multitude prior to increase; Jerusalem; restoration of Israel; Lord's disciples.[3]

When the Lord made judgment concerning the Tower of Babel he spread man across the globe into 70 nations speaking 70 different languages. One of the purposes He did this for was that the Lord had just released the flood to cleanse the world of the mixing of the natural with the supernatural. In doing so, it destroyed almost all of life on the earth. The first thing king Nimrod did was to seek after a way to kill God for having brought the flood. This includes taking on the self-proclaimed mantle of protecting the people from God trying to harm them again (thus the tower), and likewise being the world's first dictator dominating the world's entire population. This is the plan and destiny of the Devil.

Nimrod was the first human agent of the Devil, he is the beast. He and his empirical legacy is the beast out of the sea pictured in John's vision. Because of his activities, the Lord confounded the languages and dispersed humanity around the globe into 70 nations. The Lord frustrated the Devil and his beast from accomplishing its objectives at that time, restraining him from accomplishing complete global domination and thereby bringing the end of the world.

Now we see that 70 becomes a very important factor in God's salvation of mankind. After His first judgment of the flood He postpones the end by suppressing the rebellion. He does this by dividing mankind into 70 countries speaking 70 different languages. Thereby making it hard for mankind to unify into a one world government. To this date that obstacle has not been overcome. However, we know that will soon change.

After these two expressions of seventies, the Lord purifies His people, the Israelites, through 70 years of captivity in Babylon. Then through further purification of the tribulations of another 70-7 year cycles or time periods the Savior of the world is able to:

1) Enter into the world by the pure woman clothed with the sun having a crown of twelve stars (the twelve tribes of Israel).

2) Then through the purifying tribulations (birthing pains) of the same 70-7's God is able to populate heaven, bring the return of our Savior to establish His Kingdom, and wipeout evil and rebellion for all time.

The Lord promised He would not destroy the world again with a flood. As is the case He chose to use a more merciful way which causes Him to patiently suffer sinful man, until He can save for Himself a people from among the lost and rebellious. That more merciful way was the way of 70. When Peter asked Jesus how many times is he obligated to forgive his brother, is it any wonder Jesus retorted by saying I tell you 70-7 times?

NIV Mt 18:21 *Then Peter came to Jesus and asked, "Lord, how many times shall I forgive my brother when he sins against me? Up to seven times?"*
NIV Mt 18:22 *Jesus answered, "I tell you, not seven times, but seventy-seven times.*

Seven

WEB Lk 17:3 *Be careful. If your brother sins against you, rebuke him. If he repents, forgive him.* *⁴ If he sins against you seven times in the day, and seven times returns, saying, 'I repent,' you shall forgive him."*

And seven priests shall bear seven trumpets of rams' horns before the ark. But the seventh day you shall march around the city seven times, and the priests shall blow the trumpets. (**Joshua 6:4**)

In the Bible, numbers have spiritual significance. Of all the biblical numbers, seven is the most familiar because it appears about 600 times. Seven denotes spiritual perfection. It means divine fullness, completeness and totality. It comes from a Hebrew word meaning "to be full," "to be satisfied," and "to have enough."

Many times seven is important as a symbol rather than as an actual number. Whenever you read seven, it does not always literally mean seven things or seven occurrences. It is symbolic of the whole or the completion or the ideal situation or the perfect picture of things. Seven constitutes a complete cycle.

One of the most profound examples of the use of the symbolic number seven is related to the fall of Jericho in Joshua 6:1-20. Notice how many sevens appear in the Scripture above. The use of the number seven simply means fulfillment or enough. Enough priests blew the trumpets and enough people marched around the walls enough times for the walls to come tumbling down.

Revelation, the last book of the Bible that completes the word of God contains more sevens than any of the other books. There are seven churches, seven seals, seven trumpets, seven personages, seven vials, seven woes, and seven new things. Additionally, there are seven glories of the Son of Man, and seven blessings. The word "Jesus" is found seven times, "Jesus Christ" seven times and the wrath of God seven times.

In just one verse in Isaiah 11:2, the Holy Spirit rested on Jesus in seven distinct ways: Spirit of God, wisdom, understanding, counsel, power, knowledge, and fear of God. Our desire should be that the Holy Spirit will rest within us in the same seven ways.[1]

The use of 7 can best be summed up by seeing it to mean completion and perfection. God created the world in 7 days. His creation was then complete. He observed that it was good. It was perfect and perfected. It has been said about the word "good" that it is an extension of God, or what comes out of God, this is why it has two "o's" instead of one. And Jesus said only God is good. When a cycle of 7 is complete, then the 8th day is the new beginning of a new cycle.

Notes

[1] Joseph, G. N. (2008, December 25). *Biblical Numbers:1-10.* Retrieved October 2012, from Turnback to God: http://www.turnbacktogod.com/biblical-numbers-1-10/

[2] Parsons, J. J.(n.d.). *The Letter Ayin.* Retrieved October 2012, from Hebrew from Christians:
http://www.hebrew4christians.com/Grammar/Unit_One/Aleph-Bet/Ayin/ayin.html

[3] Breathitt, B. L. (2007). 70 Ayin. Dream Symbols, 1(www.myonar.com). Breath of the Spirit Ministries.

CHAPTER 2

The Structure of Sevens

How the meaning of seven applies to the book of Revelation

The framework of the book of Revelation is the **_structure of sevens._** Through the use of sevens we can know the entire scope of every prophecy in Revelation. It is the same for the seven letters to the seven churches which in turn tells us the entire scope of the Church Age and the history, past and future, of that age.

The _structure of sevens_ as used in Revelation not only gives a whole different context and understanding of Church history when viewing through it, but a clarity and certainty about its future. It also gives us a confidence that there is no other knowledge which can add or detract from what is told. Because of the _structure of sevens_ we can find the beginning, the end, and a comprehensive scope of the matters it speaks about. The reason is the meaning of the number seven is divine perfection and completion.

To know the "sevenness" of something means you understand a comprehensiveness of its perfection from beginning to end. Knowing that means we can search a matter Revelation speaks about and discover a context and a meaning of what is said which reveals the beginning and end of the matter. This is very important when it comes to Biblical interpretation. They both (the beginning and end) are in what is said even if it is hidden. The _structure of sevens_ guarantees that. The best extra Biblical information can do is to color or fill in details, even give witness to the words of the Bible. However, nothing can give hidden or additional information outside of the scope which is told through the _structure of sevens._

Outlining everything in Revelation according to its sevenness is such an important key in understanding the prophetic history, past and future. In addition, it is important to keep in mind that the use of sevens in Revelation is not just symbolic.

Perhaps it is not symbolic at all but is representative. God in His creative power and by design has actually ordained history to unfold according to the patterns of the *structure of sevens*. So the sevenness of a matter, whether it is the beginning of the universe or the end of time, will literally transpire within a structure of sevenness. In other words, when seven (or any other number for that matter) is used it does not just have a figurative or structural meaning, but a literal application as well.

The following is the meaning of prophetic history. A prophetic and spiritual understanding of history, past and future, from God's perspective and purposes is called, prophetic history. A prophet can be defined as an interpreter of the Divine will and purposes. To interpret events, history, and the future while understanding them in light of the will and purposes of God, is to give an account of prophetic history. To do so in light of human reason and will would have a completely different spin on the understanding of the same event. However, in the end, it is God, not man, who purposes, ordains, and decides all events and what their outcome serves. Below is an example of an event in history given twice, once according to secular history, and once according to prophetic history:

In the world view, history records there once was a man who caused sedition and threatened the delicate balance between the Jewish religious leaders and the occupying Roman government. He incited the people, and both the Jewish leadership and the Roman government arrested Him, and put Him to death in order to put an end to the sedition. In the eyes of the world, this man was a common criminal and suffered the consequences of disturbing the peace, breaking the law, and not aligning with His religious and secular governments. That closed the books and put an end to His sedition. That would be a secular historical account, or secular history.

The Apostles, however, gave us a different historical account and perspective. Their account is prophetic history, or a spiritual account which is framed according to the perspective and purposes of God. The same historical event according to them reads that God came down in the guise of human nature and walked among us. He voluntarily gave up His life and purposefully died, allowing them to execute Him in order that the sin of the world would be paid for, and thereby became the bridge, that man might be forgiven and finally reconciled with God. However, death did not hold Him, but He rose back to life from death three days later and now lives in the spiritual realm clothed with His celestial body. Furthermore, He still remains in the earth among men with His disembodied Spirit hosted in the bodies and hearts of His followers, continuing the very same work He did before, while unrecognizable to the people of the world.

The seven letters to the seven churches and the visions of Revelation are a prophetic history, past and future, of the world and the elect of God. As such, it needs to be read and understood through a spiritual view. It is given by God to His elect so they may be informed of all which will occur and why. In this way they can avoid every pitfall the people of the world will befall. As we go forward in Volume 2 we will examine the seven letters to the seven churches according to the *structure of sevens* to outline the past and future according to the prophetic history it reveals. Even though these seven letters were written to the seven angels of these particular churches, in the context of the *structure of sevens* this means there is a sevenness to the Church Age itself. These letters reveal the seven major turning points during the Church Age from the beginning of it, to the end, and there ensuing consequences. Just as with:

- The seven days of creation in Genesis tells us what transpired on those seven days.
- The seven heads of the Devil and of the beast reveals the seven different kingdoms of Babylon and what will transpire during those kingdoms.
- The seven seals tell us what happens from the beginning of the judgment of fire to the end. Outlined with seven God intervening turning points.
- The seven trumpets and their corresponding bowls tell of the outpouring of God's wrath and what will transpire during it.

Again, the seven letters cover the sevenness of the entire Church Age and breaks it down so we know the seven major turning points concerning the Church within its Age. Its sevenness gives a four dimensional look (which is beyond time) at the information the letters contain that they would not otherwise speak of. To look at them in a way to discover the sevenness of what they communicate is to search out the true and full meanings of the seven letters. In doing so, it will give new eyes concerning what and how we understand both the past, and the future, complete up to the end of the physical universe, and beyond.

The seven letters, which were written to the seven angels to the seven churches, are to be understood according to the *structure of sevens;* as everything else is in Revelation.

All seven letters were written to all the churches and to ALL seven Church Ages. That is from the time it was revealed to John until the very end of the Church Age.

Why did Jesus pick those particular seven churches? Because those seven churches were representative of the issues and consequences of all of the Church ages. Just as what happened on each of the seven days of creation, the things addressed concerning these seven churches are the issues and consequences of the seven ages of the Church.

Is Jesus saying there are only seven significant issues or ages in the Church? He encapsulates all of the significant issues into seven categories (so to speak), just as with the seven seals. Similarly, Jesus divides the entire history of the Church (past, present, and future at the time He gave John this vision) into seven ages. The order Jesus wrote to those particular seven churches is significant as well. Reason being, the seven Church ages correspond with the concerns for those seven churches in the order they were written.

Let us look at Daniel and the 70-7's to see how God designs and unfolds His judgment within the *structure of sevens.*

A week of days are 7 days, a week of years are 7 years. Our counting system is a base 10 system. In a similar way, when organizing and structuring, God uses what can be referred to as a base 7 numbering system. Daniel has 70 weeks of years. That is one week of years or one 7 year period times 10. This equals 70 weeks of years or 490 years. As such, we have 3 Hebrew numbers in use concerning the judgment and redemption of God's plan.

- There is 7 which means divine perfection and thoroughness or completion.
- There is 10 which means the number of perfection or completion of God's "divine order." It is the only one of the perfect Biblical numbers in which humans have a part. It is the number of completion based on God's order and human responsibility. Humans have a responsibility towards, a role in,

and experience the unfolding of God's perfect plan of judgment and redemption.

- There is 49 or 490 (49 to the 10th power). According to the base 7 system, 7 weeks of years (or a 7 year period) times 7 equals 49 years. At the end of the 49th year begins the 50th year. That year is called "the Year of Jubilee." As with the end of every 7 year period, there is a year of rest. The ground is not planted in order to give it rest, just as after 7 days there is a Sabbath when God rested from creation and humans are to rest from their labor. So there is a rest after a week of days, then again but a more comprehensive rest after a week of years (7 years), then still yet even a more comprehensive rest after 7 weeks of years (49 years).

At the conclusion of the 49th year, there is not a day but a year of rest. During that 50th year you may not sow or reap even from the plants which grow on their own. It is a time where all debts which are owed are forgiven, slaves and prisoners are set free, and properties which have been sold or used as payment for debt are returned to the original family.

At the end of the 70-7's there too is not just a Sabbath rest and a time of jubilee, but "The" Sabbath rest and time of jubilee. It is the return of Christ when He will rule the earth for 1,000 years. That truly is the time of restoration, forgiveness, and a returning of the lands to all of Israel as they gather back to their homeland from all the nations after the 7th trumpet sounds and Jesus calls them like the roar of a mighty lion.

A normal time of jubilee after the conclusion of 49 years (during the 50th) last one year, then in the 51st year the cycle begins again. However, when this jubilee to the 10th power comes, it will be for 1,000 years, which is both the judgment and redemption of God. Not during, but after the 490 years are completed, there will be one week of years when the judgment of God is poured out on the world. That one week of years or that 7 year period will be split in two.

The first half or first 3-1/2 years God's judgment will primarily be poured out on the *Church Corrupt*, whereas the second half, or the final 3-1/2 years of that week of years, judgment and punishment will be geared towards the punishment of the world who harmed His elect. After that single week of years the Christ will return, subdue the entire earth, and bring with Him His restoration lasting for 1,000 years.

After that, the finality of the judgment of all humanity who ever lived will take place by the universe first being thrown into the lake of fire. Then, all the dead (all the disembodied souls in the history of humanity) will be embodied once again—resurrected. This is in order to face the judgment seat of God. On that day, the last day of the universe, everything in creation will come to its conclusion, every natural element which comprises the physical matter in the universe will melt in the flames with a thunderous crash. The humans which were in it from its beginning to its end will either, likewise, be thrown alive into the lake of fire experiencing death (disembodiment) for a second and final time. Or they will be granted a celestial body and will live for eternity in the celestial/spiritual realm, in fellowship with God. For the natural realm will no longer exist.

As we go further we will see how the Church Age and its sevenness (the seven letters) fit into the 70-7's God decreed as told to us through Daniel. However, we will first look a little closer at the 70-7's. The 70 -7's or 490 years are broken down into three different and separate time periods; 7-7's; 62-7's; and 1-7:

NIV Da 9:24 "Seventy 'sevens' are decreed for your people and your holy city to finish transgression, to put an end to sin, to atone for wickedness, to bring in everlasting righteousness, to seal up vision and prophecy and to anoint the most holy.

NIV Da 9:25 "Know and understand this: From the issuing of the decree to restore and rebuild Jerusalem until the Anointed One, the ruler, comes, there will be seven 'sevens,' and sixty-two 'sevens.' It will be rebuilt with streets and a trench, but in times of trouble.

NIV Da 9:26 After the sixty-two 'sevens,' the Anointed One will be cut off and will have nothing. The people of the ruler who will come will destroy the city and the sanctuary. The end will come like a flood: War will continue until the end, and desolations have been decreed.

NIV Da 9:27 He will confirm a covenant with many for one 'seven.' In the middle of the 'seven' he will put an end to sacrifice and offering. And on a wing of the temple he will set up an abomination that causes desolation, until the end that is decreed is poured out on him."

NIV Da 12:10 "...Many will be purified, made spotless and refined, but the wicked will continue to be wicked. None of the wicked will understand, but those who are wise will understand.

NIV Da 12:11 *From the time that the daily sacrifice is abolished and the abomination that causes desolation is set up, there will be 1,290 days.*
NIV Da 12:12 *Blessed is the one who waits for and reaches the end of the 1,335 days."*

In order to see the 70-7's through the *structure of sevens* (prophetic history) we have to go back to the beginning of the Babylonian Empire under Nebuchadnezzar. There are so many proposed models of how the 7-7's and 62-7's work in an effort to make the end of the combined periods be when Jesus is crucified, and begin with the issuance of the decree to rebuild Jerusalem. First off, there were three different decrees issued by the Persians to allow the Jews to return and rebuild the Holy City and the second temple.

536 BC King Cyrus defeated the Babylonian Empire and the Persian Empire began (just as Daniel's vision said it would). At the defeat of Babylon, Cyrus made a decree in the same year which allowed 50,000 Jews to return to Jerusalem to resettle it, rebuild it, and rebuild the temple.

522 BC Darius I, the successor of Cyrus, made a new decree because the work on the temple had stopped. With the urging of Haggai for the work to resume Darius I made this new decree.

Under Ezra, the work once again stopped because of a decree which saw the Jews as a threat. Some of the unfinished work which had been done was destroyed as a result.

457 BC. Artaxerxes I (after being consulted by Nehemiah) issued a third decree which allowed the work to resume, the walls to be completed, and for the Jews to self-govern.

Most models want to use this third decree because when you add up the two periods of sevens (7-7's and 62-7's) you get 483 years. Starting from the time of the third decree 483 years later lands you within two or three years of the baptism of Jesus. The baptism of Jesus was partial fulfillment of the first two periods of sevens which it was said Jesus must be anointed in that time. His baptism was that anointing.

NIV Da 9:24 "*Seventy 'sevens' are decreed for your people and your holy city to finish transgression, to put an end to sin, to atone for wickedness, to bring in everlasting righteousness, to seal up vision and prophecy <u>and to anoint the most holy.</u>*"

WEB Mt 3:13 *Then Jesus came from Galilee to the Jordan to John, to be baptized by him. ¹⁴ But John would have hindered him, saying, "I need to be baptized by you, and you come to me?" ¹⁵ But Jesus, answering, said to him, "Allow it now, for this is the fitting way for us to fulfill all righteousness." Then he allowed him.*

First off, although this kind of makes everything fit neatly going forward from the third decree as the starting point of the first two periods of sevens. However, we are told that the death of Christ is what brings the close of the 69-7's. Additionally and most importantly, this interpretation doesn't work going backwards. This would mean from the fall of Babylon marking the end of the captivity you would have to add another 79 years to the 70 years that Jeremiah prophesied resulting in a total of 149 years of captivity. This would negate Jeremiah's prophecy of 70 years of captivity and additionally skew the *structure of sevens*.

Secondly, if Daniel says: *NIV Da 9:25* ". . . From the issuing of the decree to restore and rebuild Jerusalem. . ." Why wouldn't he mean the first decree? He did not say from the issuing of the third decree . . . Besides, the second two additional decrees were more about resuming work and gaining more freedom as a nation than having to do with being released from captivity and to begin the work of restoration. This model really is just trying to take events and make the numbers work, instead of using the numbers properly.

However, going by the first decree at 536 BC then adding 483 years (7-7's and 62-7's) it lands you about 79 years short of the anointing (baptism) of Jesus as the Holy One. Under conventional thinking this will not work because this seemingly destroys the *structure of sevens* also.

The following is a very important factor that will allow the structure of sevens to work.

The clue is within the prophecies of sevens. Most models of 7's out there want to run the first two periods of sevens concurrently. If they are concurrent that makes them not two periods of 7's, 7-7's and 62-7's but one period of 69-7's. Daniel is told they are separate periods of 7's, as is the last 7 from the combined 69-7's. In other words, it is alright, even necessary, to have a separation of time between the first and second 7's as is between the second and third or final 7. If you let there be a pause between the first two 7's, then all the dates and math works to the year! This makes sense because the first two periods of 7's are exactly that; divided from each other as separate.

Before we show how that works out, we have to expose another problem on the beginning side of the 7's. That is: if the 70 years in captivity ends when Cyrus conquers Babylon and issues the decree allowing them to return and rebuild, going back 70 years doesn't work either, most would say. They would argue, the first deportation into captivity and fall of Jerusalem happened in 597 BC. The second and final fall of Jerusalem, when it was destroyed completely, and everyone was taken to Babylon was in 588 BC. If you count backwards from the time of the decree of Cyrus 70 years, both these dates fall short and don't make up 70 years.

Some who want that to work would scratch their heads and figure that because of Daniel's fasting and repentance the time of 70 years in captivity could have been shortened because of an answer to his prayer. This too is just a crunching of the numbers in order to somehow make them work.

Here is the second factor that solves that problem. Jeremiah's prophecy of 70 years must be looked at more closely:

WEB Jer 25:9 behold, I will send and take all the families of the north," says Yahweh, "and I will send to Nebuchadnezzar the king of Babylon, my servant, and will bring them against this land, and against its inhabitants, and against all these nations around. I will utterly destroy them, and make them an astonishment, and a hissing, and perpetual desolations. [10] *Moreover I will take from them the voice of mirth* (laughter) *and the voice of gladness, the voice of the bridegroom and the voice of the bride, the sound of the millstones, and the light of the lamp.* [11] *This whole land* (meaning: the whole middle east area including Egypt) *shall be a desolation, and an astonishment; and these nations shall serve the king of Babylon seventy years.* [12] *"It shall happen, when seventy years are accomplished, that I will punish the king of Babylon, and that nation,"* says Yahweh, *"for their iniquity, and the land of the Chaldeans; and I will make it desolate forever.*

The 70 years the Lord is declaring through Jeremiah is not talking about the time period of captivity of the Jews so much as He is talking about the 70 years of power He is giving to His servant Nebuchadnezzar and the Babylonian Empire over the region of the Middle East. This begins when he ascends to power by conquering the nations surrounding Jerusalem, including Egypt at 606 BC. And ends 70 years later when Cyrus of Persia conquers Babylon and issues a decree for the Jews to return and rebuild.

Jerusalem had been paying tribute to Egypt. In 606 BC Babylon defeated Egypt marking the beginning of their empire and beginning the clock of the 70 years Jeremiah predicted; the 70 years that Jerusalem and the nations around them would serve Babylon.

At that time, and even though Jerusalem itself was yet to be destroyed, they began paying tribute to Babylon instead, serving them, exactly as Jeremiah foretold. In addition to them paying tribute to Babylon, items of gold from the temple were taken, and many of the princes of Jerusalem were carted off into captivity to Babylon to serve Nebuchadnezzar in his court.

This is before thousands of Jews were exiled to Babylon. Among those princes taken into captivity were included 15 year old Daniel, Hananiah, Mishael, and Azaria. Who were given the new Babylonian names of Belteshazzar to Daniel and Shadrach, Meshach, and Abednego to his three friends.

What this means is we solved the 70 year problem and the *structure of sevens* holds true as well as, the accuracy of prophecy in the Bible. 606 BC marks the year the

Babylonian Empire came to power and Daniel was brought into captivity and Jerusalem began to serve Babylon.

Starting from 606 BC, 70 years later in 536 BC marks:

1) The end of the 70 year reign the Lord had allotted for Babylon.

2) The 70th year Daniel himself had been in captivity.

3) The year Cyrus decrees the Jews can return and rebuild Jerusalem.

4) The year the 7-7's (49 years) begin.

Here are the dates:

- 606 BC to 536 BC are 70 years of exile (for Daniel and many others), and the time of power granted to Nebuchadnezzar's Babylon.

- 536 BC to 487 BC is the 7-7's or 49 years. During which time the original decree was made to release the Jews, rebuild the temple and Jerusalem. During that time they were rebuilt in a makeshift way with streets and a mote against overwhelming adversities and obstacles.

- 487 BC to 401 BC is the gap between the 7-7's and the 62-7's. The significance of this time period are unknown to the authors.

- 401 BC to 33 AD is the 62-7's or 434 years. During the time of the 62-7's the last prophet, Malachi, had spoken signaling that vision and prophecy had been sealed up. The Holy One was anointed when Jesus was baptized by John the Baptist resulting in the Holy Spirit descending upon Him like a dove. Then the Holy One is cut off—killed in 33 AD bringing a close to the 62-7's.

- 33 AD to unknown is the gap between the 62-7's and the beginning of the 1-7. So far that time period has been about 2,000 years. The significance of this gap is that it is the Church Age. It is a time for Jesus to find a bride of celestial humans for Himself by reason that the Jews have rejected that place. When the Church Age is finished the 1-7 or last seven will begin. When the 1-7 has ended it brings a close to the 70-7's, then the end comes.

The thing that is wonderful about the prophecy is we are told what will happen, and for how long we must endure things, and why we will endure them. However, at the same time, the way the prophecy is told and divides up the time when things happened makes clear to us what transpires, but at the same time we are not always told when things start. That information, Jesus told us, is not revealed, otherwise (in the words of Jesus) the owner of the house would be ready for the thief when he comes.

In other words, the way we are told about the 70-7's and the way they unfold with gaps or pauses which are not revealed, we can know just about everything we need to know about the future, except when each phase begins. How clever of God and how generous as well, that He can clue us in without spoiling His redeeming work.

What this means is if we are, for example, caught in the great tribulation we have the hope that it will only last 1,260 days (3-1/2 years) and therefore can be encouraged to hang on for a finite period of time.

As stated earlier, here is another important tool of interpretation: In the *structure of sevens*, in each vision or prophecy you can find the beginning of the matter, as well as, the end of the matter. If we continue to read Daniel we are told what happens after the 70-7's are complete when it comes to God's elect:

WEB Da 12:1 *"At that time shall Michael stand up, the great prince who stands for the children of your people; and there shall be a time of trouble, such as never was since there was a nation even to that same time: and at that time your people shall be delivered, everyone who shall be found written in the book. ² Many of those who sleep in the dust of the earth shall awake, some to everlasting life, and some to shame and everlasting contempt. ³ Those who are wise shall shine as the brightness of the expanse; and those who turn many to righteousness as the stars forever and ever. ⁴ But you, Daniel, shut up the words, and seal the book, even to the time of the end: many shall run back and forth, and knowledge shall be increased." ⁵ Then I, Daniel, looked, and behold, two others stood, one on the river bank on this side, and the other on the river bank on that side. ⁶ One said to the man clothed in linen, who was above the waters of the river, How long shall it be to the end of these wonders? ⁷ I heard the man clothed in linen, who was above the waters of the river, when he held up his right hand and his left hand to heaven, and swore by him who lives forever that it shall be for a time, times, and a half; and when they have finished breaking in pieces the power of the holy people, all these things shall be finished. ⁸ I heard, but I didn't understand: then I said, my lord, what shall be the issue of these things? ⁹ He said, Go your way, Daniel; for the words are shut up and sealed until the time of the end. ¹⁰ Many shall purify themselves, and make themselves white, and be refined; but the wicked shall do wickedly; and none of the wicked shall understand; but those who are wise shall understand. ¹¹ From the time that the continual burnt offering shall be taken away, and the abomination that makes desolate set up, there shall be one thousand two hundred ninety days. ¹² Blessed is he who waits, and comes to the one thousand three hundred thirty-five days. ¹³ But go you your way until the end; for you shall rest, and shall stand in your lot, at the end of the days.*

Previously, the 70-7's are broken down into three time periods of 7's:

- During the 7-7's or 49 years it was ordained to rebuild the city of Jerusalem by Haggai, Ezra, and Nehemiah after the decree by King Cyrus of Persia (who had taken over the Babylonian Empire after their 70 years [or 10-7's] of power).

- During the 62-7's prophecy had been sealed up with all of it made complete, some 400 years before the birth of Jesus when Malachi put his pen down. The baptism of Jesus by John (the anointing of the Most Holy) and finally Jesus was "cut-off", killed and sin was atoned for. The beginning of the 62-7's is marked by counting backwards 434 years from the crucifixion of Christ.

- During the gap between the 62-7's and the beginning of the 1-7 is the time of the Church Age. The Jews have rejected their status as the bride of Christ and from among the world He gathers to Himself a bride during this gap. We are in that gap currently.

- During the 1-7, the false prophet makes a treaty with "many". At the midpoint (3-1/2 years in) he puts an end to the animal sacrifices in the temple. The two witnesses come and give testimony, and 3-1/2 years after the midpoint the last 7 ends.

- 7 years of judgment. 75 days after the end of the 70-7's marks the beginning of the 7 years of the judgment of God. This includes 3-1/2 years of breaking the power of the holy people—the great tribulation, concluding with 3-1/2 years of punishing the world for its wickedness. The following is what happens during those 75 days leading up to the 7 years of judgment: 30 days after the 70-7's are complete, the false prophet sets up an image of the beast in the temple. Sometime within 45 days afterwards and at the height his dark magic: 1) The image rises to his feet because Nimrod, the beast and antichrist, has been called up from out of the Abyss, then is embodied with the image the false prophet made. 2) He leaves the temple and kills the unkillable, the two witness, who had just finished their 3-1/2 years of testimony. After the two witnesses had been killed, 3-1/2 days later they are raised back to life. 3) On the 45th day after the image had been set up (75 days after the end of the 70-7's and 1,335 days after the midpoint of the 1-7) the Holy Spirit withdraws from the earth taking with Him the two witnesses, who are alive again, and likewise, snatches up the *Church Pure* taking them to heaven giving them their celestial bodies. While leaving behind the *Church Corrupt* and a devastating earthquake which destroys a portion of Jerusalem and kills many. This event of the Holy Spirit leaving, marks the beginning of the 7 years of God's judgment.

- 1,000 years of heaven on earth during the Kingdom of Christ. After the 7 years of judgment are complete, there is the first resurrection, making the great multitude complete in their numbers. They are the bride of Christ and those who have become celestial humans even before the last day. In turn, with Jesus in the lead, they will follow Him to the earth with His Father, His army angels, and the New Jerusalem. The whole world will meet Jesus in battle over dominance of the globe. Jesus will destroy them all and begin His 1,000 year reign.

- After the 1,000 year reign of Christ is finished, the last day will come and the natural realm will become extinct. The dead will rise and everyone from the beginning will face the judgment seat of God.

The 70-7's are pertinent to the seven letters Jesus wrote to the seven churches in the following way:

WEB Da 12:8 I heard, but I didn't understand: then I said, my lord, what shall be the issue of these things? 9 He said, Go your way, Daniel; for the words are shut up and sealed until the time of the end. 10 Many shall purify themselves, and make themselves white, and be refined; but the wicked shall do wickedly; and none of the wicked shall understand; but those who are wise shall understand.

Daniel asks what will be the results of all these terrible events which will befall the people of God. The Lord told him to let it go because it wasn't for him to have that knowledge, nor for it to be released at that time. The Lord continued that it would be released at the times of the end.

The seven letters to the seven angels of those churches are the results which Daniel was asking about, and was not informed. Jesus tells us what He refused to tell Daniel. We are His Church and His bride, we Christians, are who these details of the Church Age (the gap between the 62-7's and the 1-7) are about, and not the Jews who rejected that place.

Verse 10 speaks about the 7 years of judgment and its results. The *Church Pure* will be removed from the earth. Through the great tribulation the *Church Corrupt* will purify themselves through their tribulations while holding fast to their testimony of Christ and refusal to worship the beast or take his mark (*many shall purify themselves*). The Jews will be hidden away in the desert at a place prepared for them by the Lord. The rest of the world will show their wickedness by killing the people of God and turning to the pre-flood evil of the demonic (breaking down the boundaries between the natural and supernatural) through Nimrod the beast and antichrist (*but the wicked shall do wickedly*). Revelation tells us of them:

Amp Rev 9:20 *And the rest of humanity who were not killed by these plagues even then did not repent of [the worship of] the works of their [own] hands, so as to cease paying homage to the demons and idols of gold and silver and bronze and stone and wood, which can neither see nor hear nor move.*
Amp Rev 9:21 *And they did not repent of their murders* (of the Church) *or their practice of magic (sorceries) or their sexual vice or their thefts.*

Again, it is during the undetermined time of the gap between the 62-7's and the 1-7 that the Church Age occurs. It is through the seven letters that we, the Church/His bride, get to see the sevenness of that gap between the 62-7's and the 1-7. God has not let that gap be a random time period before the next and last phase of His decree is executed. God, likewise, has not kept its significance from His people. No. God has, through *the structure of sevens*, shown His people exactly what will transpire with

His bride, and what will be the result. The seven letters are a prophetic history of that time period which makes it every bit as important as what happens during the 70-7's. Again, the book of Revelation is written to the Church and no others!

Structure of Sevens Timeline

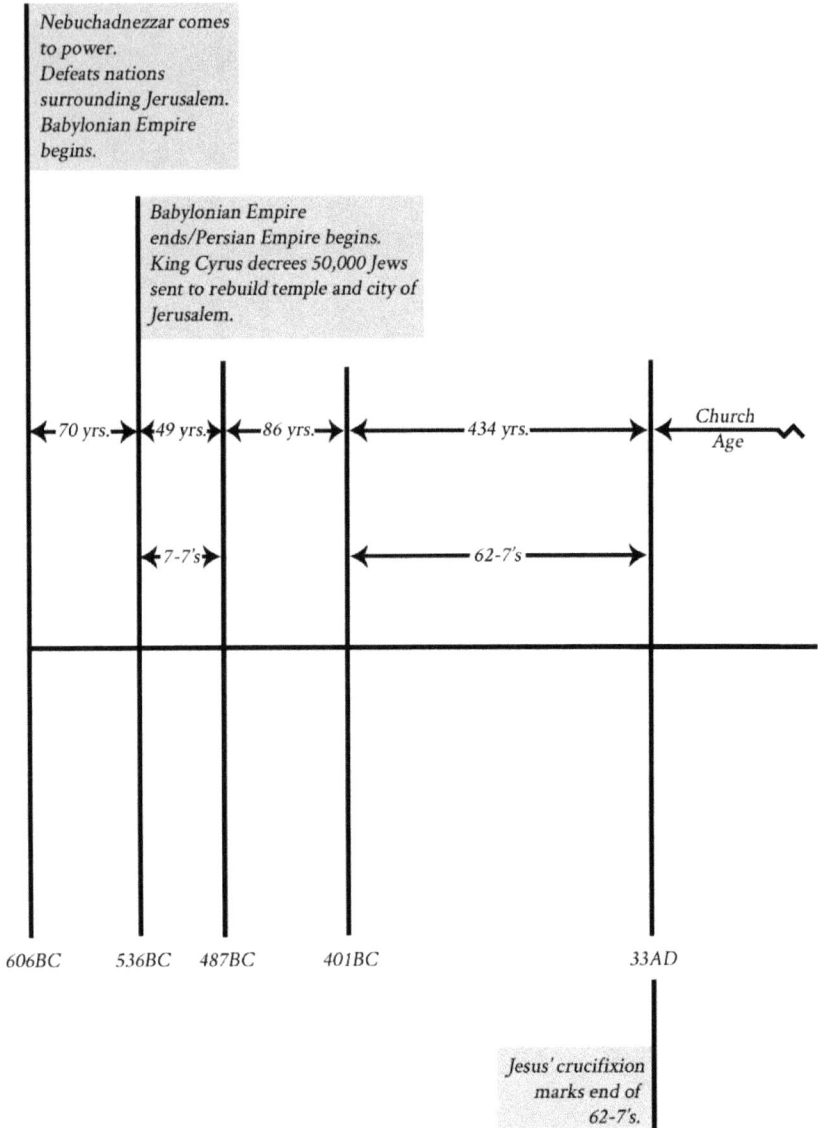

Nebuchadnezzar comes to power.
Defeats nations surrounding Jerusalem.
Babylonian Empire begins.

Babylonian Empire ends/Persian Empire begins.
King Cyrus decrees 50,000 Jews sent to rebuild temple and city of Jerusalem.

←70 yrs.→ ←49 yrs.→ ←86 yrs.→ ←————434 yrs.————→ Church Age

←7-7's→ ←————62-7's————→

606BC   536BC   487BC   401BC   33AD

Jesus' crucifixion marks end of 62-7's.

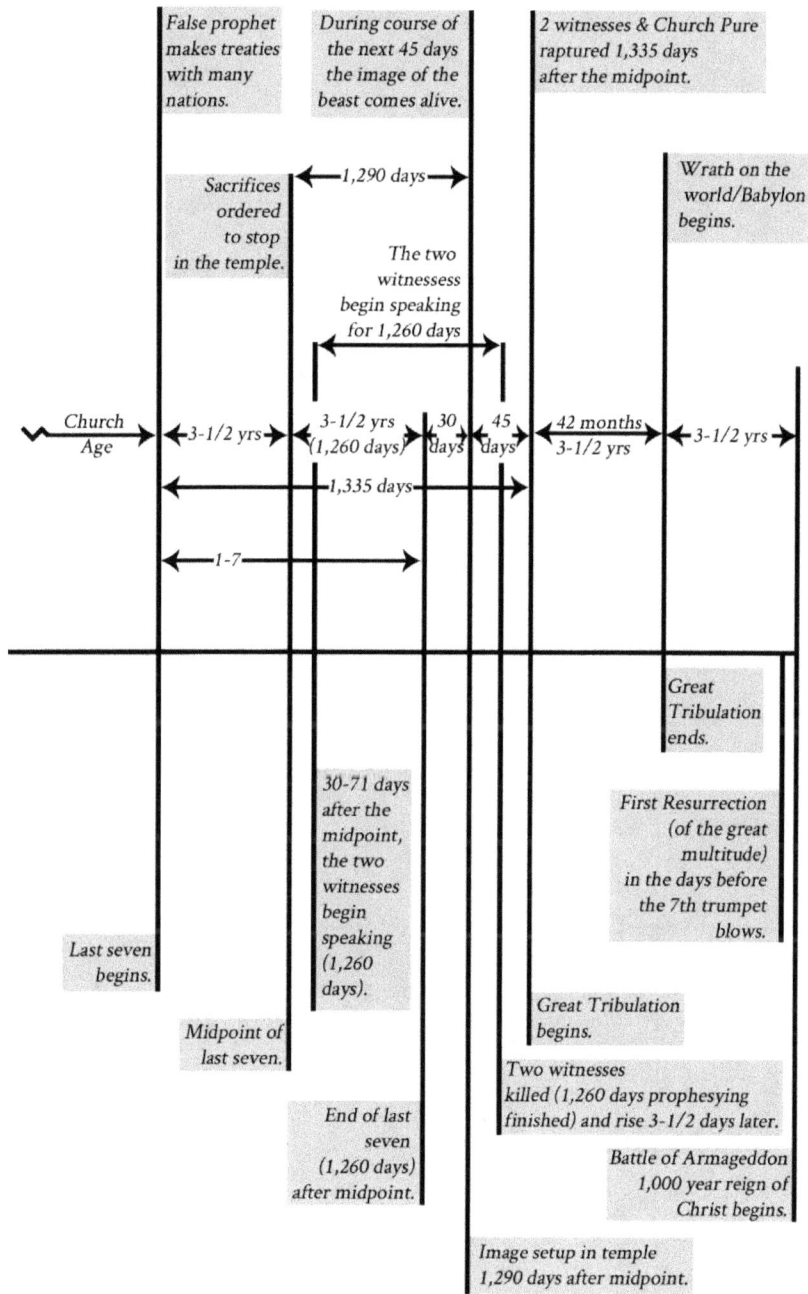

False prophet
makes treaties
with many
nations.

During course of
the next 45 days
the image of the
beast comes alive.

2 witnesses & Church Pure
raptured 1,335 days
after the midpoint.

Sacrifices
ordered
to stop
in the temple.

←1,290 days→

Wrath on the
world/Babylon
begins.

The two
witnessess
begin speaking
for 1,260 days

Church
Age

←3-1/2 yrs→

3-1/2 yrs
(1,260 days)

30
days

45
days

←42 months→
3-1/2 yrs

←3-1/2 yrs→

←1,335 days→

←1-7→

Great
Tribulation
ends.

30-71 days
after the
midpoint,
the two
witnesses
begin
speaking
(1,260
days).

First Resurrection
(of the great
multitude)
in the days before
the 7th trumpet
blows.

Last seven
begins.

Great Tribulation
begins.

Midpoint of
last seven.

Two witnesses
killed (1,260 days prophesying
finished) and rise 3-1/2 days later.

End of last
seven
(1,260 days)
after midpoint.

Battle of Armageddon
1,000 year reign of
Christ begins.

Image setup in temple
1,290 days after midpoint.

CHAPTER 3

Introduction to the Seven Letters

Written to the Seven Churches

Double-edged sword

WEB *Rev 1:9* *I John, your brother and partner with you in the oppression, Kingdom, and perseverance in Christ Jesus, was on the isle that is called Patmos because of God's Word and the testimony of Jesus Christ. 10 I was in the Spirit on the Lord's day, and I heard behind me a loud voice, like a trumpet 11 saying, "What you see, write in a book (scroll) and send to the seven assemblies: to Ephesus, Smyrna, Pergamum, Thyatira, Sardis, Philadelphia, and to Laodicea." 12 I turned to see the voice that spoke with me. Having turned, I saw seven golden lamp stands. 13 And among the lamp stands was one like a son of man, clothed with a robe reaching down to his feet, and with a golden sash around his chest. 14 His head and his hair were white as white wool, like snow. His eyes were like a flame of fire. 15 His feet were like burnished brass, as if it had been refined in a furnace. His voice was like the voice of many waters. 16 He had seven stars in his right hand. Out of his mouth proceeded a sharp two-edged (double-edged) sword. His face was like the sun shining at its brightest.*

"A double-edged sword" is important to recognize because most swords have only one cutting edge on the bottom side of the sword. But there are swords which have a cutting edge on both top and bottom. They are called a double-edged sword. They cut both ways. When using the saying of something being a "double-edged sword," it means your actions cut both ways. For example, you say, "I will kill my enemy so he does not hinder me anymore." An advisor might say, "That is a double-edged sword that cuts both ways; it might stop your enemy from hindering you but you will go to jail for it and lose your life anyway."

How does this apply to Jesus and why is it coming out of His mouth and not in His hand?

The sword coming out of His mouth are His words that cut/divide what is true from what is false. However, His words are a double-edged sword as we see in Hebrews 4:12 (below). His words expose the truth in our hearts also exposing the deception thereby giving us the ability to choose truth, leading to repentance, giving us eternal life. However, the same words that expose the truth and deception giving opportunity for repentance and life, also bring judgment and death to those who choose to hate the exposing light and run from it by not repenting. His words cut both ways, they bring life and judgment, those are the two-edges.

Amp Heb 4:12 For the Word that God speaks is alive and full of power [making it active, operative, energizing, and effective]; it is sharper than any two-edged sword, penetrating to the dividing line of the breath of life (soul) and [the immortal] spirit, and of joints and marrow [of the deepest parts of our nature], exposing (bringing life) and sifting and analyzing and judging (bringing judgment) the very thoughts and purposes of the heart.

WEB Jn 12:47 If anyone listens to my sayings, and doesn't believe, I don't judge him. For I came not to judge the world, but to save the world. 48 He who rejects me, and doesn't receive my sayings, has one who judges him. The word that I spoke, the same will judge him in the last day (bringing judgment). 49 For I spoke not from myself, but the Father who sent me, he gave me a commandment, what I should say, and what I should speak. 50 I know that his commandment is eternal life (bringing life). The things therefore which I speak, even as the Father has said to me, so I speak."

It is at this place in the letters to the seven churches that His words are spoken of as being a double-edged sword. Here to His Church they can bring life, as well as, judgment. In fact, they are spoken primarily to bring life. What we will find in the below verse is that when Jesus comes back at His second coming it is to bring justice and destroy evil, establishing His 1,000 year reign. He comes to war, judging the inhabitants of the earth and avenging the blood of the souls who formerly resided under the altar in paradise and had been slain because of the word of God and the testimony they had maintained.

NIV Rev 19:15 Out of his mouth comes a sharp sword with which to strike down the nations. "He will rule them with an iron scepter." He treads the winepress of the fury of the wrath of God Almighty.

NIV Rev 19:21 *The rest of them were killed with the sword that came out of the mouth of the rider on the horse, and all the birds gorged themselves on their flesh.*

It is interesting to note that now the sword which comes out of His mouth (His words) no longer has a double-edge. His words no longer save bringing life, rather they judge and bring death.

By this Scripture an important significance is brought to the previous sword. Especially because of the fact that the double-edged sword is said to be coming out of Jesus' mouth as He begins to dictate His words to the churches in the seven different ages. What we should understand by this is that He has many things against His Church throughout its entire history to come (that is as of the time these letters were written). Although Jesus exposes them to each Church Age and warns them, He will bring judgment on them because of what He has against them if they do not repent.

The very same words are first meant to expose our errors and sins to us so we repent and correct our errors, thereby remaining in good standing with Him. However, these very same words in the seven letters meant to save and bring life, if not acted upon, will finally judge and condemn us. He will wait until the last minute before closing the books. However, as we will see with clarity through the seven letters, judgment first comes to His people, then the rest of the world.

NIV Jn 12:46 *I have come into the world as a light, so that no one who believes in me should stay in darkness.*
NIV Jn 12:47 *"As for the person who hears my words but does not keep them, I do not judge him. For I did not come to judge the world, but to save it.*
NIV Jn 12:48 *There is a judge for the one who rejects me and does not accept my words; that very word which I spoke will condemn him at the last day.*

Amp Jn 3:19 *The [basis of the] judgment (indictment, the test by which men are judged, the ground for the sentence) lies in this: the Light has come into the world, and people have loved the darkness rather than and more than the Light, for their works (deeds) were evil.*

Amp Jn 3:20 *For every wrongdoer hates (loathes, detests) the Light, and will not come out into the Light but shrinks from it, lest his works (his deeds, his activities, his conduct) be exposed and reproved.*

Amp Jn 3:21 *But he who practices truth [who does what is right] comes out into the Light; so that his works may be plainly shown to be what they are—wrought with God [divinely prompted, done with God's help, in dependence upon Him].*

This is a very important concept. We all love to receive Jesus' Spirit into our hearts. The one thing we don't consider is that when we open ourselves up to His soothing, healing, peaceful Spirit (light), that light starts to expose things in our hearts which are in stark opposition towards God and His will. We become painfully aware of this as a result. Our motives are laid bare. The minds-sets, attitudes, outlooks, ideas, and desires which are in conflict with the will of God become, over time, fully illuminated so we cannot delude ourselves anymore. All our conflictedness and double-mindedness are brought to light. It is then—armed with this self-knowledge—that we come to a crossroad and must choose to repent and receive life, or (deny; justify; rationalize; get defensive; blame others) shrink back from the illuminating self-knowledge and bring judgment on ourselves. This is what happens when the light comes in, as Isaiah said when before the throne of God:

Amp Isa 6:5 *Then said I, Woe is me! For I am undone and ruined, because I am a man of unclean lips, and I dwell in the midst of a people of unclean lips; for my eyes have seen the King, the Lord of hosts!*

When people are highly anointed with light (the Holy Spirit) and the words they speak are from the Lord, their counsel will cut both ways. They will bring healing, peace, and life, but they will also expose and lay bare the thoughts and purposes of the heart causing us to see how although we say we love God and will serve Him, we have many ideas about life and our own agendas which prevent us from truly serving his will.

As Jeremiah spoke:

Amp Jer 23:28 *. . . he who has My word, let him speak My word faithfully. What has straw in common with wheat [for nourishment]? says the Lord.*

Amp Jer 23:29 *Is not My word like fire [that consumes all that cannot endure the test]? says the Lord, and like a hammer that breaks in pieces the rock [of most stubborn resistance]?*

To judge if a person is from God, it is not by the goose bumps and good feeling they give us, but by the peace, healing, joy, harmony as well as the illumination of our guilt and our aversion to line-up with God's will, including the denial that lets us believe we are doing God's will when it is really our own.

The seven letters are different Church ages

WEB Rev 1:17 *When I saw him, I fell at his feet like a dead man. He laid his right hand on me, saying, "Don't be afraid. I am the first and the last,* [18] *and the Living one. I was dead, and behold, I am alive forever more. Amen. I have the keys of Death and of Hades* [19] *Write therefore the things which you have seen, and the things which are, and the things which will happen hereafter;* [20] *the mystery of the seven stars which you saw in my right hand, and the seven golden lamp stands. The seven stars are the angels of the seven assemblies* (churches). *The seven lamp stands are seven assemblies* (churches).

Although these letters were dictated to John for seven of the churches of his day, Jesus picked these seven different churches because they also prophetically represented the concerns and issues of seven different Church ages. Given this is true, Jesus has divided the Church Age into seven different times or ages as was done to creation with its seven days.

Seven in the Bible is the number of perfection, completion, and fullness. In these letters we have a prophetic picture of the Church's complete history, past and future, on earth. This shines a brand new light on these seven letters!

Imagine with eyes closed for a moment, John sitting there and he turns to listen to a voice behind him—a voice so piercing, like a trumpet blast it undoes him—and he sees the magnificent sight of Jesus he described in the beginning.

John sees the seven prophetic voices for the seven ages in His right hand as stars. These seven stars are seven angels of the seven different ages of the Church. Each of these angels are assigned one of the seven messages Jesus is giving to the seven different Church ages. These angels are responsible for the release of their prospective message and keeping it present in the hearts of the elect, from the time it is released until the time it has accomplished its work. This time period will exceed that of one man's lifetime, that is why angels have been given charge of these messages.

The angels release an anointing, power, and revelation to God's prophets and teachers causing them to have an unction and a determination to speak the messages of the angels to the Church. In assigning these precious messages in the angels' charge, Jesus' messages will not die with the human voices who release expression to them. They remain alive from generation to generation as the angels inspire all those whose hearts are open to receive the words of the Lord.

John sees Jesus with eyes blazing with fire. Eyes that illuminate and expose all things before Him as He walks among the lamp stands—the churches of the different ages. He moves silently throughout time itself searching and judging the thoughts and purposes of the hearts and minds of all those in all seven of the different Church ages until His return to the earth.

John is watching this sight as Jesus instructs him to write down what is now, and to come, and to address these letters to give to the different churches in their ages to come. John will be long dead before he can deliver the messages to the seven different Church ages. This is why he is instructed to address them to the seven different angels who in turn are to be responsible to release them in their proper time and keep the words active and powerful until the end of the Church Age.

Many will question this logic and say these letters were written to the seven churches they were addressed to, and not to all the churches for all time. They argue that these letters are not prophetic. However, Jesus told John to write down what will take place in the future:

Amp Rev 1:19 *Write therefore the things you see, what they are [and signify] and what is to take place hereafter.*

Furthermore, they will question where in Scripture does it support that they are addressed to anyone other than the seven different churches that were named? Or where does it show relevance to more than what they themselves were going through at that time? John is instructed to address each letter to the angels of those churches and their ages. Secondly, Jesus requires John to send these letters to the seven churches.

NIV Rev 1:10 *On the Lord's Day I was in the Spirit, and I heard behind me a loud voice like a trumpet,*
NIV Rev 1:11 *which said: "Write on a scroll what you see and send it to the seven churches: to Ephesus, Smyrna, Pergamum, Thyatira, Sardis, Philadelphia and Laodicea."*

NIV Rev 2:1 *"To the angel of the church in Ephesus write:*
NIV Rev 2:8 *"To the angel of the church in Smyrna write:*
NIV Rev 2:12 *"To the angel of the church in Pergamum write:*
NIV Rev 2:18 *"To the angel of the church in Thyatira write:*
NIV Rev 3:1 *"To the angel of the church in Sardis write:*
NIV Rev 3:7 *"To the angel of the church in Philadelphia write:*
NIV Rev 3:14 *"To the angel of the church in Laodicea write:*

Finally, Jesus concludes each of the seven letters with this same exact statement:

NIV Rev 2:7a *He who has an ear, let him hear what the Spirit says to the churches."*

Next, as Jesus tells John to take down these seven letters, the scene in John's vision shows Jesus with the seven stars in His hand walking among the seven lampstands. It cannot be ignored that here are three sevens (seven letters, seven angels, and seven lampstands). We must remember the *structure of sevens*. Jesus is telling us through the vision that:

- Here is the sevenness of the Church from beginning to the end of its Age
- Here is the sevenness of its errors and correctness

These angels are not for just those seven different churches but are the seven different angels for the whole of the Church for all of its existence in the world.

They are the sevenness of the Lord's protection over His Church. These angels are given charge of this message for the entire Church Age. That's why it is addressed to them so they may inspire with revelation those in the Church long after John's death.

In order to understand who Jesus was really addressing by using the number seven, one needs to consider only this: "How would there be only seven churches represented by seven lampstands in heaven before God?" It is certain that there are only seven lampstands before the throne. It is also certain that there were more than seven churches when John wrote these letters and throughout history tens of thousands more. This has to mean only one thing: That all of the churches throughout history are represented in those seven lampstands.

Next: When Jesus is dictating this letter, He is walking among the lampstands.

When He does, we are told that the seven different lampstands are the seven different churches. However, later in chapter four of Revelation we are told those lampstands are the sevenness of the Spirit of God.

NLT Rev 4:5 And from the throne came flashes of lightning and the rumble of thunder. And in front of the throne were seven lampstands with burning flames. They are the seven spirits of God.

Those who receive a new spirit, are born again with the light burning in those lampstands. Within those seven lampstands is the Spirit of His bride. In those lampstands the actual Spirit of His bride, the life-principle which makes her perfect and presentable to Him, has already existed and has been burning in heaven in those lampstands awaiting the time when it would finally inhabit the hearts of the saints. The sevenness of the Spirit of the bride was perfected and contained within those seven lampstands even before God promised that the day was to come when He would give us a new Spirit:

NLT Jer 31:31 "The day will come," says the LORD, "when I will make a new covenant with the people of Israel and Judah.
NLT Jer 31:32 This covenant will not be like the one I made with their ancestors when I took them by the hand and brought them out of the land of Egypt. They broke that covenant, though I loved them as a husband loves his wife," says the LORD.

NLT Jer 31:33 *"But this is the new covenant I will make with the people of Israel on that day," says the LORD. "I will put my laws in their minds, and I will write them on their hearts. I will be their God, and they will be my people.*

NLT Jer 31:34 *And they will not need to teach their neighbors, nor will they need to teach their family, saying, 'You should know the LORD.' For everyone, from the least to the greatest, will already know me," says the LORD. "And I will forgive their wickedness and will never again remember their sins."*

And again:

NIV Eze 11:19 *I will give them an undivided heart and put a new spirit in them; I will remove from them their heart of stone and give them a heart of flesh.*

NIV Eze 11:20 *Then they will follow my decrees and be careful to keep my laws. They will be my people, and I will be their God.*

That Spirit existed even before the creation of the world, and was awaiting that day to leave the lampstands and inhabit His people, His bride:

NIV Eph 1:3 *Praise be to the God and Father of our Lord Jesus Christ, who has blessed us in the heavenly realms with every spiritual blessing in Christ.*

NIV Eph 1:4 *For he chose us in him before the creation of the world to be holy and blameless in his sight. In love*

NIV Eph 1:5 *he predestined us to be adopted as his sons through Jesus Christ, in accordance with his pleasure and will—*

NIV Eph 1:6 *to the praise of his glorious grace, which he has freely given us in the One he loves.*

This is how it is true that we were predestined even before the foundations of the world to be His bride. Jesus knew us before we were born. However, He knew us by spirit because in those lampstands which were in front of Him even before there was the first man, our Spirit as His bride were already created and perfected. Since we are spirit, soul, and body, Jesus only lacked the heart (personality/mind) and faces of the people who would embody that Spirit of the bride. God then made man with the spirit of Adam, the first man. And out of the human race we have Esau and Jacob.

Esau, was the first born. And the two wrestled with each other in the womb. Jacob came second clutching Esau's heal (Ge 25:22-26).

WEB Ge 3:15 *I will put hostility between you and the woman,*
and between your offspring and her offspring.
He will bruise your head,
and you will bruise his heel."

Esau, the hunter, was jealous for strength and power in the world he was created in. Jacob was jealous not for the world he was created in, but for the spiritual promise of the world to come. God created the human race, which fell. Out of the human race there are those who do not want strength and power in the world they were born in, but want the spiritual promise of the world to come. God gives the Holy Spirit to the latter to be born again with.

Here is the point, in those seven lampstands burning with life is the sevenness of the Holy Spirit. For those who, like Jacob, want the promise of things to come, that Spirit will be transferred to their hearts and will be embodied by them. When the Spirit of the bride inhabits the full number of His bride, the lampstands will no longer burn with the Spirit. All those who as one constitute the bride will then embody the fullness of those seven Spirits blazing and they will no longer occupy the lampstands! As such, in those seven lampstands Jesus is seen walking among while dictating these seven letters, He is studying the entirety of His Church from its beginning to its end and speaking towards the sevenness of its existence before He returns to them. Yes, those letters are not only meant for the seven churches of John's time, but for the entire Church body. They will become born again and embody the fullness of the Spirit in those seven lampstands Jesus walks among and studies.

Note: The constant use of seven is so conspicuous that it is obvious that to understand Revelation, you have to understand the purposes of seven and what it represents. Without factoring in the purposes of the use of seven, there is no way one can believe he has an accurate interpretation of Revelation. It's like putting together a bicycle and having a handful of extra parts and then throwing them away believing they are not necessary because you don't know how they are used. That is until you get halfway down the road and the wheels fall off. The most important function of the use of seven has to do with how what is said is encompassed, outlined, and structured.

Understanding John's vision through the scope of the *structure of sevens* will give proper context and aid to interpret the seven letters revealing the times for which they are meant! Since these letters are written according to the *structure of sevens*, it means we see the order that each error comes to the Church throughout history As well, we see the results these errors have on the Church accumulating to the end of the Church Age. Like yeast, the errors work their way through the whole Church throughout all the eras of the Church ages.

As Jesus tells us through the seven letters the errors which will separate us from Him as the Church Age progresses, He also informs us that He sends the seven angels at just the right time to illuminate the errors that creep in. This results in the prophetic voices in the earth those angels inspire. That is so when these men speak throughout history, we can know in advance that they are speaking for Jesus and calling us out of error. By giving us these seven letters in advance, He is qualifying His prophetic voices beforehand, making their message one we can trust when they speak things against the direction of the entire Church, seemingly going against Church authority.

This is a huge advantage because it is hard to trust and not condemn those who speak against the Church or its established authority. This is especially important for the fifth and sixth Church ages when the Lord admonished His Church to "wake up" and "remember" or suffer the consequences. It is during these two ages the angels of those ages rose up mighty prophets who gave their lives to call the people out of the *Church Corrupt*, out of Babylon. That was in addition to these men giving the sacred Scriptures back into the hands of the common people so they might search out for themselves what the *Church Corrupt* had suppressed and finally lost. Without the Lord prequalifying these voices who exposed and condemned the Roman Church through these letters, it would be a difficult thing to believe the evil that exists within the authority of the Church.

Instead, the history of the Church shows us that they didn't recognize how Jesus has qualified His prophetic voices to the Church by the seven letters He sent long before. The fact is, they don't recognize the message in the seven letters as affirmation of the prophetic voices to come, those prophetic voices were thought of as wrong for condemning the Church and speaking against it. They have been called heretics, and usurpers of authority for coming against the sins of the Church, speaking against its leaders, and dividing from them. We have killed them and tortured them. To name a few, John Wycliffe, John Huss, Martin Luther, John Calvin, John Wesley, and George Fox.

Jeremiah had this same issue. He was from God but said things against God's people. For example, God will give Jerusalem over to the enemy and let them be carried off. But the people said he was crazy and that God would never let the Holy City and the Holy Temple be destroyed and given over to evil people. Clearly, God was warning His people through His prophet Jeremiah, but they did not listen.

The Church has done the same to the saints and the prophets who have come to speak God's message. Since the Church has not listened to the seven letters and have rejected God's messengers, correcting the Church's errors, they have compounded their sins in a way that has divided them from God. Taking on the religion of Cain, they fool themselves into thinking they are in union with Christ and are doing His work.

Errors Entering into the Church

Jesus warned us through the seven letters given to John of major errors coming into the Church. In addition, at just the right time, He ordained each one of His seven stars to come and expose them as they happened. We can look at these major errors as like cones of errors, in that throughout Church history, errors have been introduced into the Church at a certain starting point and through a single source. As the cones of error extend themselves throughout Church history they grow wider in scope and influence. Jesus likened the same thing with the corrupt leaders of the Jews as "yeast" which works its influence through the whole batch of dough. We see throughout history that although there are some who heed His warning and separate themselves from the errors in question, those cones of error, nevertheless, continue to grow higher in time and wider in scope of influence. Then, the next major error enters in beginning a new cone of error.

The first cone of error doesn't stop as we enter into the succeeding Church age, but continues to grow until the end of the entire Church Age, while facilitating the next cone of error. However, these cones of error that influence the Church throughout its age actually divides the *Church Pure* from the *Church Corrupt*. Not just on the outside as if one denomination or type of church is better than the other. But more importantly, in the individual hearts of the people from within the different kinds of church buildings and denominations. It is a spiritual separation that places one inside of the cone of error of the *Church Corrupt* or outside the cone of error in the *Church Pure*, and not so much the different buildings they attend or the different denominations.

That's not to say that church leadership and the many denominations have not been corrupted by the influence of these errors Jesus admonishes us about. The fact is, according to Jesus, they have been profoundly influenced by them causing the Church itself to stray from "the way." However, the Church will be judged and suffer its destruction as the prostitute during the great tribulation. Likewise, we will be judged individually as those given over to the corrupt ways of the churches we belong to.

Amp Rev 18:4 *I then heard another voice from heaven saying, Come out from her, my people, so that you may not share in her sins, neither participate in her plagues.*

Amp Rev 18:5 *For her iniquities (her crimes and transgressions) are piled up as high as heaven, and God has remembered her wickedness and [her] crimes [and calls them up for settlement].*

Amp Rev 18:6 *Repay to her what she herself has paid [to others] and double [her doom] in accordance with what she has done. Mix a double portion for her in the cup she mixed [for others].*

Amp Rev 18:7 *To the degree that she glorified herself and reveled in her wantonness [living deliciously and luxuriously], to that measure impose on her torment and anguish and tears and mourning. Since in her heart she boasts, I am not a widow; as a queen [on a throne] I sit, and I shall never see suffering or experience sorrow—*

Amp Rev 18:8 *So shall her plagues (afflictions, calamities) come thick upon her in a single day, pestilence and anguish and sorrow and famine; and she shall be utterly consumed (burned up with fire), for* mighty is the Lord God Who judges her.

That is also not to say that there are within each individual church those who belong to the *Church Corrupt* and those who belong to the *Church Pure*. However, the Lord warns us to disassociate ourselves from them and change our ways from their ways. The Lord faces us with the fact that the Church will grow in its corruption all the way to the end when Jesus divorces the *Church Corrupt* and spews it out of His mouth. This is something set in stone and will not be changed. He informs us of this in the seventh letter to the seventh church. The result of His, "spewing us out of His mouth" will be the Church left on earth to endure the great tribulation.

Then one might ask, what's the difference? How will we avoid the punishment against the Church during the great tribulation? All Christians, good and bad, will suffer during that time. The answer is that you can escape those times altogether by being separated from the corruptness of the Church. If you are, you will not even be present during that horrific time, but in the spiritual realm clothed with a celestial body in direct fellowship with the Father and the Son. You will be snatched up in the rapture the very day the great tribulation begins.

We will see when we read the seven letters that each error builds upon the earlier ones. Each error widens the scope of the influence of the previous consuming a larger and larger percentage of individuals into the *Church Corrupt*. This occurs until basically there are "few" in the *Church Pure* when the Church Age comes to an end. At which time, the overwhelming majority of individuals are in the *Church Corrupt*. They are senselessly doomed to suffer the great tribulation. All of which could have been avoided if only they had listened to His warnings in these seven letters to His Church. This is not a doom and gloom teaching like the contemporaries of Jeremiah thought he was. This is the admonishment of Jesus Himself who has eyes of blazing fire, who walks among the seven lampstands, to the seven churches in their seven ages, as we will see below.

CHAPTER 4

Ephesus

The First Church Age

To the Church in Ephesus

WEB Rev 2:1 *"To the angel of the assembly* (church) *in Ephesus write:*
"He who holds the seven stars in his right hand, he who walks among the seven golden lamp
stands says these things: [2] *"I know your works, and your toil and perseverance, and that you*
can't tolerate evil men, and have tested those who call themselves apostles, and they are not,
and found them false. [3] *You have perseverance and have endured for my name's sake, and*
have not grown weary. [4] *But I have this against you, that you left* (forsaken) *your first love.* [5]
Remember therefore from where you have fallen, and repent and do the first works; or else I
am coming to you swiftly, and will move your lamp stand out of its place, unless you repent. [6]
But this you have, that you hate the works of the Nicolaitans, which I also hate. [7] *He who has*
an ear, let him hear what the Spirit says to the assemblies (churches). *To him who overcomes*
I will give to eat from the tree of life, which is in the Paradise of my God.

Who were the Nicolaitans?

The word "Nicolaitans," in Greek, means "followers of Nicolas." The name "Nicolas"
means "victor of the people." Hippolytus of Rome states that the deacon Nicolas was
the author of the heresy and the sect. Several of the early church fathers, including
Irenaeus, Epiphanius, and Theodoret mentioned this group. Irenaeus discusses them
but adds nothing to the Apocalypse except that "they lead lives of unrestrained
indulgence." Victorinus of Pettau states that they ate things offered to idols. Bede
states that Nicolas allowed other men to marry his wife and Thomas Aquinas
believed that Nicholas supported either polygamy or the holding of wives in
common. Eusebius said that the sect was short-lived. Epiphanius relates some
details of the life of Nicolas the deacon, and describes him as gradually sinking into
the grossest impurity, and becoming the originator of the Nicolaitans and other
libertine Gnostic sects: [Nicolas] had an attractive wife, and had refrained from
intercourse as though in imitation of those whom he saw to be devoted to God. He

endured this for a while but in the end could not bear to control his incontinence....
But because he was ashamed of his defeat and suspected that he had been found out,
he ventured to say, "Unless one copulates every day, he cannot have eternal life."

—Epiphanius, Panarion, 25, 1[4]

"They seem to have held that it was lawful to eat things sacrificed to idols, and to
commit the immoral excesses of the heathen, in opposition to the decree of the
Church rendered in Acts 15:20, 29. Mingling themselves in the orgies of idolatrous
feasts, they brought the impurities of those feasts into the meetings of the Christian
Church Lovefeast. And all this was done, it must be remembered, not simply as an
indulgence of appetite, but as a part of a SYSTEM, supported by a "doctrine,"
accompanied by the boasts of a prophetic illumination" (p.449).[5]

They tried bringing those heathen practices to the Lovefeast of the Christian
community convincing everyone that it was a new revelation from God that they
should.

*NIV Jude 1:10 Yet these men speak abusively against whatever they do not understand; and what
things they do understand by instinct, like unreasoning animals—these are the very things
that destroy them.*
*NIV Jude 1:11 Woe to them! They have taken the way of Cain; they have rushed for profit into
Balaam's error; they have been destroyed in Korah's rebellion.*
*NIV Jude 1:12 These men are blemishes at your love feasts, eating with you without the slightest
qualm—shepherds who feed only themselves. They are clouds without rain, blown along by
the wind; autumn trees, without fruit and uprooted—twice dead.*

In order to have a comprehensive meaning to these errors of the Nicolaitans we have
to go back in history to Nimrod. He started a form of worship eventually called Baal
worship. The idol was a representation of a penis called an obelisk. They
fellowshipped together drinking and feasting and having unbridled sex. The temple
priestesses prostituted themselves for this god as a part of the worship practice. This
form of worshiping was copied by the Egyptians, Greeks, and the Romans as well as
many others. It is this type of practice which many converts to Christianity were
formally involved in. As a result, many who struggled with sin would often try to
corrupt the Christian Lovefeast by trying to introduce these practices.

Lovefeast was the form of Christian fellowship where a community of believers
would gather, sometimes daily, eat a meal together, worship God through songs,

psalms, and testimonies of God by all who attended; instead of just a single preacher teaching a message. They would end the evening by having communion. Some would try to seduce others at the Lovefeast into sexual activity in the name of love. And some would claim special knowledge and give supposed prophetic words claiming God had instructed them to incorporate sexual practices as a part of their worship in order to justify their own corrupt desires and to seduce others to do the same. The Gnostics similarly believed that Jesus saved the soul, but the body is doomed to death. That the body is corrupt. They decided it was alright to do whatever they wanted (pleasure wise) because the body is not saved and they thought what they do in the body has no effect on the soul's salvation.

The Nicolaitans were one such group. Some churches were seduced by these sinful ways, and others tolerated the practices of them being too weak to stop them. The Lord praised this church, that at least they hated the impure ways of those who would pollute and corrupt the virtue at their Lovefeasts. Likewise, they were not seduced by those who claimed they had "special knowledge" and were "apostolic" endorsing the indulgence of such practices.

Note: At close look, a pattern can be seen in how Jesus structures these letters to the different churches. He first states something to identify Himself. It is usually a pertinent attribute of His which has to do with something He is trying to emphasize to the church He is writing to. He points out the things of this church He is in favor of. He states what He holds against them and what He is warning them against. He next will speak the ultimate outcome of what His blazing insight admonishes. That is what the outcome will be if the Church takes heed, and what it will be if they do not. We refer to this as His double-edged sword which cuts both ways in that His words can be a blessing, or a judgment depending on how we respond. Finally, He reminds them of the attributes He possesses which bring power to the words of admonishment He speaks to them.

If we were to take these letters as being written and meant only to the seven different churches they were addressed to, they are not much good for us 2,000 years later, other than to possibly glean something from their mistakes. However, in order to understand the sevenness of the entire Church Age, past, present, and future, and its prophetic history, we must look at these seven letters in a context which opens our eyes to the prophetic history they tell. In an effort to do just that, we have broken down each letter zeroing in on:

- What He says **for** them
- What He says **against** them (and/or **warns** them about)
- What He says revealing each side of His **double-edged sword**; words which give **life**, and words which **judge**.
- **The characteristics of His person** He describes to bring power to His words.

The First Church Age

For: *"I know your works, and your toil and perseverance, and that you can't tolerate evil men, and have tested those who call themselves apostles, and they are not, and found them false. You have perseverance and have endured for my name's sake, and have not grown weary."*

"...But this you have (for you), that you hate the works of the Nicolaitans, which I also hate."

Against/warning: *"...you left (have forsaken) your first love."*

What is meant by, "you have forsaken your first love?" It is a much more serious issue than just: we prefer/love things in the world over Jesus. For example, "I prefer to watch the game during football season instead of going to church on Sunday, that can't be a sin, right?" That preference is the resulting symptoms of losing your first love.

To behold Jesus as your first love means, you are dead to self and alive in Christ. To forsake your first love means, you are no longer dead to your life in the body and alive as the body of Christ. This is a result of having had taken up your life again and wanting to carry out your own desires, will, and life agendas. We call this shift, "switching grails!" Our quest, once again, becomes about pleasing ourselves and chasing after our own pursuits in life. This happens instead of being on a quest to live for Jesus and carry out His will at the expense of not being able to carry out our own.

When this happens we are truly deceived and it is a worse state than when we were in the world. Why? Because we knew we did not do the will of God when we were in the world, but did our own. When losing our first love and switching the grails we seek after, we do it in delusion. We still talk the same as if our quest is the same and we still seek the Lord's will to live for Him. However with a twist; we want His will to be what ours is. So when they don't match up (our will and His) we question and create doubt. We require affirmation of His will, questioning His promptings until they line up with our own. All the while saying, I will do His will if I know what it is. In this state, we no longer diligently and objectively seek out His will. We instead, inundate God with requests for things to go the ways we want them to. With our zealousness gone to seek out His will on a matter, we merely wait on God to break into our constant stream of requests (prayers) to tell us what He wants us to do. If He doesn't, we continue to live for what we desire until that moment comes.

Jesus speaks directly towards these circumstances:

Amp Jn 7:17 If any man desires to do His will (God's pleasure), he will know (have the needed illumination to recognize, and can tell for himself) whether the teaching is from God or whether I am speaking from Myself and of My own accord and on My own authority.
Amp Jn 7:18 He who speaks on his own authority seeks to win honor for himself. [He whose teaching originates with himself seeks his own glory.] But He Who seeks the glory and is eager for the honor of Him Who sent Him, He is true; and there is no unrighteousness or falsehood or deception in Him.

Jesus' wisdom is so sound, yet profoundly basic. He is saying that if in your heart you desire first and most importantly to do the will of God above concerns for your own life and interests, then what seems right to you will indeed be the will of God. That is even if you do not hear an audible voice or see prophetic visions. Conversely, if in your heart your desire is to do your own will, being primarily concerned with your own life and interests, then what seems right to you will be your own will. As a result, it then follows that your own desires will witness to you as the will of God.

Furthermore, if you have at heart to do the will of God and do the work He wants accomplished, you will truly represent God and there is no falsehood or deception (self-deception or otherwise) in your motives, words, or actions. However, if you have at heart to do your own will and accomplish your own agendas, even if you are representing God like the Jewish leadership Jesus was speaking this to, you will be self-deceived, and false to the truth. As such, you will not actually speak or act for God. To want in priority to do God's will above your own in your heart of hearts is for Jesus to be your first love. To have at heart a desire to do your own will and carry out the agendas you desire, or to protect your own life and interests, is to embrace yourself as your first love and as a result you have "lost your first love."

To lose your first love often deteriorates into the attitude of, "what is He going to ask of me next?" His will start interfering with our purposes and pursuits. We search for ways and through Scriptures to find how it could not possibly be His will to do what our conscience is telling us. We make pre-decisions like "I could never do this if God asked me." As a result, God sadly already knows our answer before He asks something from us. We stop hearkening to God, meaning our focus is no longer fixed on having a sense of God and what He desires for us to do. We become focused on our own desires. We are then reduced to constantly asking Him to arrange things so that we get what we want. Simply put, we stop seeking His will out and focus on our own.

We twist things around in our prayer life like the guy who says to God, "if there is a parking spot right in front of the door to the donut shop, then I know it is your will that I can have a donut." Low and behold there is a parking spot right in front of the donut shop and he takes it as affirmation God wants him to have a donut. However, just to make sure, he had to go around the block four times before a parking spot actually opened up.

These are the symptoms of one who has lost their first love because their desires and priorities have shifted from Jesus to self, all while they still talk and act like they are serving Him. This first departure from the true path is the most fatal one. For it is on this error all other errors and deceptions are easy to be snared by. We then reason that it isn't our fault, but that it was an innocent mistake, or that we were seduced or deceived into doing wrong.

However, the losing of our first love is a personal choice and preference that we make. It is out of that wrong preference that allows us to be seduced and deceived into doing wrong or mishearing God. Our deception and seduction is our own fault and it is as W. C. Fields says, "you cannot cheat an honest man." If you have the proper heart and Jesus is your first love in preference and priority, then you will not be deceived or seduced into deception and error, even if you do not understand and are naive. For the Holy Spirit, who is our righteousness and our wisdom from heaven, will guide us through our conscience.

Note: In our contemporary church it is sad to say the greatest majority of Christians have never forsaken their first love, rather most have never learned to serve Jesus as their first love. They never grow out of their immaturity into a mature Christian.

When we are children it is all about everyone doing for us, and that is the proper order of things. However, when we grow as an adult we mature into a person who lives larger than themselves and it becomes about what we can contribute to others. It is the same with our Christianity. In the beginning, God makes everything go our way and saves us from our circumstances. However, like becoming an adult, it is expected that our Christianity matures and we start living beyond ourselves for God. This is real relationship—a proper love relationship.

The pitfalls outlined above of someone's outlook who has lost their first love is the only thing most Christians have ever known or were modeled. Consequently, they think this is what it means to be a Christian because of the self-centered sin nature within us not maturing into embracing God above self. They may have been born again, however, they have not died to self. They can never say about themselves:

WEB Ga 2:20 I have been crucified with Christ, and it is no longer I that live, but Christ lives in me. That life which I now live in the flesh, I live by faith in the Son of God, who loved me, and gave himself up for me.

Why call this losing your first love? It says in the Bible to make our requests known, and we will receive what we ask for. Or, "Following Jesus that way is not for everybody but only for extreme people that He calls with huge destinies." "Jesus knows I love Him and I obey Him in my own way!" . . . Some may argue.

When is the honeymoon over in a marriage? It is when your love for your spouse is reduced to being loyal and faithful to your shared life together, however, you begin to desire to pursue personal space and time independent from your spouse. This causes one's focus to shift from constantly seeking out what would please their spouse (having as a priority to anticipate and discover what would please them and pursue that), to wanting personal desires and having mostly in mind what pleases self.

Eventually, this shift in focus that happens in that place beyond words begins to make it somewhat of a burden to please the other over self. Then progressively, if left unchecked, pleasing the other and serving one's common life instead of self turns into something to contend with. It is as Jesus said, you cannot serve two masters. You will love the one and hate the other. You will serve and honor the one at the sacrifice of not doing so for the other. Marriage and your spouse becomes a ball and chain. On the other hand, as long as you are faithful and loyal to your marriage and spouse while contributing to its survival, it is thought of as being loving because you have done your duty in the marriage. However, your passion grows cold over time and serving the other becomes something to contend with, instead of a labor of love. Paul too compares *spiritual union* with Christ to union in a marital relationship:

NIV Eph 5:28 *In this same way, husbands ought to love their wives as their own bodies. He who loves his wife loves himself.*
NIV Eph 5:29 *After all, no one ever hated his own body, but he feeds and cares for it, just as Christ does the church—*
NIV Eph 5:30 *for we are members of his body.*
NIV Eph 5:31 *"For this reason a man will leave his father and mother and be united to his wife, and the two will become one flesh."*
NIV Eph 5:32 *This is a profound mystery—but I am talking about Christ and the church.*
NIV Eph 5:33 *However, each one of you also must love his wife as he loves himself, and the wife must respect her husband.*

Being loyal, doing your duty, and contributing to your common life together, while pursuing self-interests and having your own space, may keep you bound together superficially. However, when it comes to *spiritual union*, to have independent desires and pursuits is to divorce oneself from that union, even if you are loyal doing your duty, and contributing to that relationship. This is the case because of the very nature of *spiritual union*.

Spiritual union is for the two to become together one whole person. Two souls, inspired and moved by the one's spirit, expressed through the other's body. To forsake one's own desires and pursuits, then instead to respond and obey the promptings of the Spirit of Christ in you, is the only binding strap which make the two one—one whole person with Christ.

To love Christ and have intimacy with Him is to obey Him. To be moved by the Lord's Spirit promptings is an act of intimacy which by nature further binds you to Him in *spiritual union*. Likewise, to do that, is to hold Him as your first love. To break free by living for self-interests and to carry out personal desires, is to break those binding straps which make you together one whole person with Christ. That is to lose your first love and to make yourself your first love. This is the case even if one is a loyal Christian going to church, doing his duty, and contributing to God. To do the latter is to practice a (Christian) religion just as the Jews have their religion.

NAS LK 16:13 *" No servant can serve two masters; for either he will hate the one and love the other, or else he will be devoted to one and despise the other*

These words are true, to serve one purpose automatically makes another purpose something to contend with because it is in the way of accomplishing the one you hold in priority. When the Bible uses words like hate and love it means much more than an emotion or attitude towards someone. To love someone is an action, and that action would be to nurture and care for a person. When we are told to love our neighbor as our self, it is asking of us to do the same for them as we would do for our very own bodies. If we are cold we love ourselves if we then clothe our body. If we are tired we give it rest. If we are hungry, we feed ourselves. If we are hurt we bind up the wounds on our body. The commandment saying to love our neighbor is to care for him as we would our own bodies; if they are hungry feed them, if they are in need give to them.

Whereas hate is also an action. John tells us that if we see a brother cold and we own two coats but tell him we will pray for him that God provides, we hate our brother. To hate in a Biblical sense, is to not nurture, even to be neglectful of the needs of another when we have the means to help.

To hold self as our first love means we will hold as the most important priority, to carry out our own desires and to satisfy our own needs. However, you can only hold one thing to be your number one priority by serving its needs. This is because in the end, to serve the priorities of the one is to neglect the priorities of the other. To serve the one is to love that one (your first love), however, to serve that one is at the expense of neglecting or hating the other.

This is a truth: if we do an act that God needs done, but we do it because it accomplishes something for ourselves, then what we have done serves our own purposes and accomplishes something for us. As such, it does not serve the reason God needed it to be done, even though it was done. One might think, "That's not true! I was killing two birds with one stone!" "I was serving God by furthering my self-interest."

Moses was asked by God to speak to the rock so it would pour out water for the Israelites. Moses struck the rock out of anger at the people because they were hostile, grumbling against him, and blaming him. To strike it demonstrated his anger and a superiority or control over them. However, God provided the water from a rock and asked Moses to do it representing Him, in order to quiet the fears of the people and show them they could trust God to take care of their needs. Moses performed the task God asked of him, and it quenched the thirst of the people. However, in doing this "God" task, Moses served his own purpose bringing glory to himself. He used the act to demonstrate to the people his disdain over them. Meanwhile, the purpose of God went unfulfilled, which was to show His compassion and care for their lives. It is for this reason Moses was unable to enter the Promised Land.

This is exactly why Jesus told us we must hate our lives in this world and pick up our cross and follow Him. We must at the expense of neglecting our own self-interest and needs, serve His. Thereby we give His Spirit expression through our life in the body. The day we stop doing that is the day we break free from the binding straps of oneness with Christ. Likewise, it is the day our Christianity becomes a religion and no longer a *spiritual union*. Jesus started out by telling this church that they have been loyal, faithful and have persevered, but they lost their first love. This is not unlike the husband who is loyal, faithful, and perseveres to honor his marriage, but then redirects his heart by wanting to do his own thing within the boundaries of being loyal to his marriage.

In their superficial and unspiritual thinking people who have lost their first love are the hardest to help see their error. They cannot even see how it is true when in their minds they give their due to God. This situation is not unlike the fellow who sits in the bar drinking with his workmates late every night and gets angry because his wife calls and is upset trying to persuade him to come home to her. He hangs up and complains to his friends, "I give her my paycheck every week, I build a beautiful home for her, I take out the trash, clean the garage and take the boys to little league, what the heck more does she want from me?" She wants you . . . She wants to be your first love in both preference and priority, like she was in the beginning . . .

The double-edged sword, life and judgment:

Words that give life: *"He who has an ear, let him hear what the Spirit says to the assemblies. To him who overcomes I will give to eat from the tree of life, which is in the Paradise of my God."*

The words that give judgment: *"Remember therefore from where you have fallen, and repent and do the first works; or else I am coming to you swiftly, and will move your lamp stand out of its place, unless you repent."*

Jesus is right to ask us to remember the height we have fallen from because when we switch grails, forgetting our first love, the new state of our heart begins to feel normal. We forget what it was like when we reconciled our life as dead and only considered in our minds His will, hearkening to Him, and not giving mind or thought to what we would want. Only a good shepherd can help his sheep see about themselves when they have lost their first love. It is such a subtle shift in what is most important to us, however, people continue to speak in the same fashion as they did when they had their priorities straight.

"... repent and do the first works; or else I am coming to you swiftly, and will move your lamp stand out of its place, unless you repent." According to the nature of *spiritual union*, it is an act of spiritual adultery, even divorce when we have abandoned our first love (which is *spiritual union* with Christ) and therefore are in spiritual adultery. As such, Jesus judges in this case that if we do not repent of our unfaithfulness, He will divorce us by taking away our lampstand. Let us remember, Jesus Himself said this is the one reason someone can divorce his spouse (Mt 19:8)— marital unfaithfulness.

To take away our lampstand, is to take away the Holy Spirit from within us. He did it to the Jews causing Him to pursue us, the Gentiles. Why would He not do the same to us for the same sin of spiritual unfaithfulness—the losing of our first love? This all is in line with the saying of Jesus when He spoke to the final Church age that He is planning to spew us out of His mouth (Rev 3:16). Also, what Jesus meant when speaking the parable about the talents (Mt 25:14-30).

NIV Mt 25:28 " 'Take the talent from him and give it to the one who has the ten talents.
NIV Mt 25:29 For everyone who has will be given more, and he will have an abundance. Whoever does not have, even what he has will be taken from him.
NIV Mt 25:30 And throw that worthless servant outside, into the darkness, where there will be weeping and gnashing of teeth.'

This church of Ephesus represents the very first Church age. Losing our first love is the first error of which separates us from our New Covenant relationship with the Lord. The rest is just religious practices, or the keeping to a morally good code of conduct. The binding straps which keep us one with the Lord are broken when we no longer live for His Spirit promptings, but for our own desires and life choices. From this error every error can creep in and seduce us. To lose Jesus as our first love causes us to forget what it means to be in a New Covenant relationship with Christ, which reduces us to relate to Christ strictly in a religious or morally good way.

However, to do so is to completely invalidate and make of no effect the very thing which saves us from having to experience death making us celestial humans (the

New Covenant relationship with Christ). That leaves us in a position like the Jews! Which means we will have to die becoming disembodied and be held captive in the paradisiacal place in Hades awaiting the last day. Then hopefully be judged as sheep becoming a celestial human and avoid the second death. This means (for all intents and purposes) that Jesus died for nothing in our individual case, if this is how and when we have the opportunity to receive salvation. Truth be known, Jesus died and experienced death primarily so that we would not have to experience death ourselves.

Note: What is described above does not take away the fact that Jesus' death as a sacrificial lamb paid for the sin of the world. However, His major purpose in doing so was to die for us so that we ourselves would not have to die. His blood was shed and He died to pay the price so we would not have to experience death. This is a literal happening and not a clever cliché that represents something as the modern Church has turned it into.

There is, however, one other way to still achieve bride status and avoid waiting until the last day. That is to participate in the first resurrection. Even in this scenario we must still experience death and Hades but will be resurrected when Jesus comes into His Kingdom. However, there is a strict criteria to be part of this group. First of all, you need to live during and endure the great tribulation. Secondly, you must not come off your testimony of Christ, not worship the beast, nor take his mark even under the threat of death.

It should not go without noting that this error of losing your first love takes place in the very first Church age. We need look no further than the Bible and the letters the Apostles wrote to the churches to see how this is true. The Epistles were repeatedly about correcting the issue of losing our first love. Paul was the "undisputed champion" (as the saying goes) who fought his whole Christian life to protect those of the faith from losing their first love, and from altering our understanding of how salvation comes through a New Covenant relationship with Christ.

What this tells us is that the Church has, from its beginning, this propensity to want salvation, however, not want to die to self and live instead for Christ. As the old proverb goes, "you can't have your cake and eat it too." However, they wanted their cake, and to eat it too. That is to be lovers of themselves first, before lovers of God. The Church from its beginning has always (in large part) constantly wanted to relate to God in a manner which says, "give me some moral rules to live within and let me live my life, fulfilling my own desires, while I make sure I don't offend or sin against You." Here is how Paul warned Timothy to be wise against this trend:

NLT 2Ti 3:1 You should also know this, Timothy, that in the last days there will be very difficult times.

NLT 2Ti 3:2 For people will love only themselves and their money. They will be boastful and proud, scoffing at God, disobedient to their parents, and ungrateful. They will consider nothing sacred.

NLT 2Ti 3:3 They will be unloving and unforgiving; they will slander others and have no self-control; they will be cruel and have no interest in what is good.

NLT 2Ti 3:4 They will betray their friends, be reckless, be puffed up with pride, and love pleasure rather than God.

NLT 2Ti 3:5 They will act as if they are religious, but they will reject the power that could make them godly. You must stay away from people like that.

Verses 4 and 5 (above) bear repeating, here they are again (below) in a different translation:

ASV 2Ti 3:4 traitors, headstrong, puffed up, lovers of pleasure rather than lovers of God;
ASV 2Ti 3:5 holding a form of godliness, but having denied the power there of. From these also turn away.

The characteristics of His person to this church: *"He who holds the seven stars in his right hand, he who walks among the seven golden lamp stands says these things"*

Jesus reminds them that He has the power to remove their lampstand! You can't fool Me, I know what is in your heart—what your top priority is.

Amp Lk 14:26 If anyone comes to Me and does not hate his [own] father and mother [in the sense of indifference to or relative disregard for them in comparison with his attitude toward God] and [likewise] his wife and children and brothers and sisters—[yes] and even his own life also—*he cannot be My disciple.*

Amp Lk 14:27 Whoever does not persevere and carry his own cross and come after (follow) Me *cannot be My disciple.*

Amp Lk 14:28 For which of you, wishing to build a farm building, does not first sit down and calculate the cost [to see] whether he has sufficient means to finish it?

Amp Lk 14:33 So then, any of you who does not forsake (renounce, surrender claim to, give up, say good-bye to) all that he has cannot be My disciple.

Amp Lk 14:34 Salt is good [an excellent thing], but if salt has lost its strength and has become saltless (insipid, flat), how shall its saltness be restored?

Amp Lk 14:35 It is fit neither for the land nor for the manure heap; men throw it away. He who has ears to hear, let him listen and consider and comprehend by hearing!

Notes

[4] *Nicolaism.* (2014, January). Retrieved October 2012, from Wikipedia, The Free Encylopedia: http://en.wikipedia.org/wiki/Nicolaism

[5] Dankenbring, W. (n.d.). *Who are the "Nicolaitans".* Retrieved October 2012, from TriumphPro.com: www.triumphpro.com/nicolaitans.htm

CHAPTER 5

Smyrna

The Second Church Age

To the Church in Smyrna

WEB Rev 2:8 *"To the angel of the assembly* (church) *in Smyrna write:*
"The first and the last, who was dead, and has come to life says these things:
⁹ "I know your works, oppression, and your poverty (but you are rich), and the blasphemy of
those who say they are Jews, and they are not, but are a synagogue of Satan. ¹⁰ Don't be afraid
of the things which you are about to suffer. Behold, the devil is about to throw some of you
into prison, that you may be tested; and you will have oppression (persecution) *for ten days.*
Be faithful to death, and I will give you the crown of life. ¹¹ He who has an ear, let him hear
what the Spirit says to the assemblies (churches). *He who overcomes won't be harmed by the*
second death.

". . . you will have oppression persecution for ten days." We have already talked about numbers and how they hold more than numeric meaning. When there is a number of things in a dream or vision it is the spiritual meaning of the number most often than the numeric value. However, God has a way of working in the numeric value so that it too is significant. We already saw how the number seven means certain qualities and not necessarily amounts. However, most often in Revelation they mean both.

It is the same with the number ten. For ten days you will suffer and be persecuted. Ten doesn't work for days, however, it does work for years, among other things. This is not beyond how God uses or encrypts timing. He does the same thing with other measurements. For example, at one point in Revelation, Jesus calls a week of years (seven years) an hour. It was in reference to the ten kings who will have (what He called) their hour of power.

NIV Rev 17:12 *"The ten horns you saw are ten kings who have not yet received a kingdom, but who for one hour will receive authority as kings along with the beast.*

A week of years is a complete cycle or a unit. An hour is a complete cycle or unit. So the Lord has encrypted a unit of seven (years) by saying a unit of minutes which is an hour. Likewise, we also hear in Revelation in regards to this same "hour" or seven year time period, that heaven was silent for about a half an hour.

NIV Rev 8:1 *When he opened the seventh seal, there was silence in heaven for about half an hour.* *NIV Rev 8:2* *And I saw the seven angels who stand before God, and to them were given seven trumpets.*

In this case, the verses (above) are referring to the identical seven year time period which he called an hour. What this tells us is heaven will not intervene in the affairs of the world. It will be "silent" or inactive "about half an hour," (three and one half years) out of the "hour" (seven years), that the ten kings have their reign. What both these verses are covertly referring to is the global desolation (which is the absence of the presence of God and His Spirit in the world) known as the great tribulation. It will last for half of a week of years, a half an hour, or a half of a seven—three and one half years.

Then the next verse reads that seven angels were given seven trumpets. That is descriptive of how heaven will once again become active and no longer silent. No more of the elect will be allowed to be harmed from this point forward. Conversely, the sevenness, the perfect, complete, and comprehensive punishment of the world (who persecuted the Lord's elect) will now commence for the second half of that hour of power. In other words, for three and one half years hell will rain down on the entire globe as it did in Egypt against Pharaoh with Moses. Just as the Israelites of that time who were not affected by those plagues, the surviving elect will have a mark from God which will not allow them to be harmed by the plagues of their time.

The use of ten in Revelation is one of the most fascinating usages of a number. The Lord has done the same with the number ten as with "one hour" of power. In this case, the main meaning of "ten days" is referring to ten reigns of power by different Roman Caesars. One day equals one reign of an emperor. There were ten emperors who persecuted the Christians thus there were ten days of persecution. He also has encrypted a period of ten years by saying ten days, likewise, the way 10 is used, we will see, fits a few other representations at the same time. However, as stated before, the Lord's use of the number ten has a much deeper meaning than its literal numeric aspect. There is a "tenness" which has to be fulfilled in order for the Lord's plan for salvation to be complete and perfect. As with all prophecy, the tenness which gives its literal account in a quantity of years revealing a regional and contemporary expression of this prophecy, also has an end times and global expression. While searching this dimension of tenness we will discover the full prophetic meaning of the tenness Jesus writes to us about. As this study progresses we will see exactly how the tenness of our relationship with the Lord and our salvation has its beginning and its end throughout the entire Church Age.

Instead of only having the future to look at in understanding the fulfillment of the tenness of the words of Jesus we, in these contemporary times, have history to show us how these prophetic words took shape in the past. John wrote Revelation and this letter to the angel of the church in Smyrna in 96 AD. At that time Jesus predicted "you are about to suffer . . . " 207 years after Jesus dictated these letters to John there came a time from 303 AD to 313 AD which was known as "The Diocletianic Persecution" or "The Great Persecution." As noted by the dates above this lasted for a ten year period.

There were ten edicts made in the Roman Empire that brought persecution on the Christians. As noted above there were ten emperors of Rome who persecuted the Christians. This is the reason the Lord referred to the Roman persecution as ten days. He was counting the reign of each emperor as a day, or their day of power. Thus, ten days; ten different reigns of emperors who persecuted the Christians.

The tenth and last of these emperors was the most notable and the most cruel towards Christians. During his twenty year reign as emperor, the last ten years was the most horrific time the Christians of the Roman Empire were forced to endure. Diocletian's reign of terror against Christians gave way to the bliss and prosperity of the next emperor, Constantine. It was Constantine who brought that ten years of persecution to an end in 313 AD through the Edict of Milan.

It is plain to see that the number ten has both symbolic and numeric meaning. It would be a mistake to believe that these occasions of ten, "the ten days of persecution" Jesus is referring to is the total fulfillment of His words. There must be an end times and global fulfillment of Jesus' prophetic word. He called each of the reign of ten different kings, or emperors a "day." That would put the emphasis on the reign of the king, or the king himself who will do the persecuting. However, we have to consider these ten succeeding kings as the regional and contemporary expression of this prophecy. When, then, will be the end times expression of this prophecy? That is to say, what will be the end times and global fulfillment of it? Was it after the tenth emperor who perpetrated the persecution and did so for ten years? The answer lies within the visions of both the beast and of the Devil. It is the ten horns of which they both possess in the vision.

NIV Rev 12:3 *Then another sign appeared in heaven: an enormous red dragon with seven heads and ten horns and seven crowns on his heads.*
NIV Rev 12:4 *His tail swept a third of the stars out of the sky and flung them to the earth.*

NIV Rev 13:1 *. . . And I saw a beast coming out of the sea. He had ten horns and seven heads, with ten crowns on his horns, and on each head a blasphemous name.*
NIV Rev 13:2 *. . . The dragon gave the beast his power and his throne and great authority.*

We see in the verses above that it was from the garden, when the Lord decreed the destiny of both Eve and the Devil and the enmity between them, that the end of time should result in this persecution of one line of offspring by the other. We see how ten kings (horns or powers) will rule the entire globe during the time of the antichrist. Verse 12:4 tells us that one third of the Christians of that time will be killed by the Devil, through the antichrist and his ten kings who rule the world.

"His tail swept a third of the stars out of the sky and flung them to the earth." Contrary to popular belief, a third of the stars in the sky flung down to the earth, represents the killing of the elect, and not the corruption of one third of the angels in heaven who join the Devil. Calling the elect, stars in the sky represents the heavenly stature of the Christians. Their stature reaches to the heavens. It is from the heavens that their spirit shines down to the earth through their earthly body illuminating the world with spiritual insight and power. When it says the Devil flung them down to earth, it is referring to their body going in the earth to their graves, leaving their heavenly spirit, no longer able to shine in the earth through them.

How will the Devil accomplish this mass genocide? Verse 13:2 above tells us. The Devil gives his power to the beast to carry this out, and the beast or antichrist entrusts it to the ten global leaders of the earth he lords over. We hear more details of this explained in the verses below:

NIV Rev 17:12 "The ten horns you saw are ten kings who have not yet received a kingdom, but who for one hour will receive authority as kings along with the beast.
NIV Rev 17:13 They have one purpose and will give their power and authority to the beast.
NIV Rev 17:14 They will make war against the Lamb, but the Lamb will overcome them because he is Lord of lords and King of kings—and with him will be his called, chosen and faithful followers."
NIV Rev 17:15 Then the angel said to me, "The waters you saw, where the prostitute sits, are peoples, multitudes, nations and languages.
NIV Rev 17:16 The beast and the ten horns you saw will hate the prostitute. They will bring her to ruin and leave her naked; they will eat her flesh and burn her with fire.
NIV Rev 17:17 For God has put it into their hearts to accomplish his purpose by agreeing to give the beast their power to rule, until God's words are fulfilled.

The prostitute is the *Church Corrupt* who has empowered herself by becoming the 7th kingdom of Babylon. They are the ones left behind after the rapture and will endure the great tribulation. The verses above tell us that God had granted this power to the antichrist in order that His words will be fulfilled. The purpose being that in their martyrdom the *Church Corrupt* can be purified, becoming celestial humans and the great multitude who will rule with Christ for a thousand years.

For the tenness of our relationship with God and our salvation to become complete, the worst suffering is yet to come. The ten horns or kings who will come into their hour of power during the three and one half years of the great tribulation will impose this suffering onto the Christians. Again, these ten horns refers to how the entire globe will be divided into ten kingdoms given to ten kings under the beast. The emphasis being ten kings simultaneously persecuting the elect. During the reign of these ten kings the persecution of Christians will be global and not just in the territories of the Roman Empire. Even more so, it will not be confined to the church of Smyrna. It will result in the imprisonment and persecution of countless numbers and the death of one-third of the Christian population, worldwide.

What this means is the symbolic meaning that ten has, which applies to the persecution of Christians, has multiple numeric occurrences until it blossoms into its global/end times manifestation. That is to say when we finally have the global persecution perpetrated by the ten kings who reign over every area of the globe, it is then that the prophecy given to Smyrna will be fulfilled.

Note: Here is a very clear example of how Jesus is not just talking to the seven different churches, but simultaneously to the seven different Church ages—the entire history of the Church. It is only through understanding His use of the number ten that we can see how this is true.

Here is some more insight into the symbolic meaning of ten that will help us understand the tenness of persecution. Ten means fullness of time, or completeness. The number ten in Hebrew message: if we are humble, God's hand can direct our lives so that we can return and live with Him again. Thus, Ten Commandments to follow. Likewise, the ten days of testing by the Devil can humble us so the Lord can save us. This works nicely for how ten is used here because Revelation is about how God will use martyrdom as a means of purifying His elect. However, they must be martyred while standing on their testimony so they may be accepted in His Kingdom forever. God will save them but they have a responsibility to make the tenness of their salvation complete and perfected.

In Volume 1 we learned that there are four numbers of completeness and perfection, three, seven, ten, and twelve. Three means: divine perfection/completeness. Seven means: spiritual perfection/completeness. Twelve means: governmental perfection/completeness. Ten is a number of perfection and completeness of God's divine order. It is the only one of the perfect Biblical numbers in which humans have a part. The Ten Commandments are an example of God's order and man's responsibility. In regards to persecution, it is part of God's plan/order to purify His bride and it is man's responsibility while He is doing this, to hold true to his testimony of Jesus, not worship the beast or take his mark. Even at the cost of his life. These two things working together, God and man doing their respective parts, make the bride perfect and complete, clean and without blemish. The verses below speak of this process even for the case of Jesus, the first born and our Savior:

NIV Heb 5:7 During the days of Jesus' life on earth, he offered up prayers and petitions with loud cries and tears to the one who could save him from death, and he was heard because of his reverent submission.

NIV Heb 5:8 Although he was a son, he learned obedience from what he suffered

NIV Heb 5:9 and, once made perfect, he became the source of eternal salvation for all who obey him

NIV Heb 5:10 and was designated by God to be high priest in the order of Melchizedek.

Ten signifies: testimony, law, responsibility. It is important to note that the meaning of ten incorporates testimony and responsibility. It was already stated that when it comes to the perfection of ten, it is the only number of perfection in which man has a role or a responsibility towards it to be complete. As a part of the tenness of the Church Age it is those who hold fast to their testimony in Christ while not worshiping the beast or taking his mark (even at the forfeiting of their lives) who will take part in the first resurrection and the second rapture. As a result, they will become celestial humans who reign with Christ for 1,000 years. This is our role or responsibility during the tenness of the persecution of the elect during the Church Age and specifically, during the time of the beast, the great tribulation.

Ten is also like saying in our day, there were a million of them, or, to the tenth power. The usage of ten in this respect works too, in the sense that ten reflects there will be persecution to the tenth power. Or there will be a countless number of them. Or a comprehensive amount of persecution. It was not just the Roman Empire that has persecuted Christians. Christians have historically been persecuted, they are now and will be, right up until the end. However, it is the struggle between the line of offspring of the Devil and the antichrist, versus the line of offspring from Eve and the Christ, by which judgment and redemption comes to man.

Completeness of order, marking the entire round of anything is, therefore, the ever-present significance of the number ten. It implies that nothing is wanting; that the number and order are perfect; that the whole cycle is complete, lacking nothing. This use of ten again matches up nicely with this definition of ten. That is because God is granting the persecution for His purposes and He will allow it to happen only as much as is needed to fulfill His will. No less and no more. Perhaps by using ten in this light, God is saying that there will be no meaningless persecution, only what is necessary to bring about our salvation.

This is confirmed when it is asked: How long before God will judge the world against the killing of the saints? They who asked are told to be patient until the fullness of their brothers are killed.

The persecution of the church of Smyrna reflects or foreshadows what will take place during the end times, and global expression of the tenness of the persecution of the worldwide Church. Here is a brief article that talks about the persecution that happened to the church of Smyrna and the affect it had on the Christian faith.

> . . . From this, Satan learned a great secret; Persecution will not stamp out the Church of the Lord Jesus. Consequently, the age ended with the easing of persecution; then Satan used what turned out to be one of the most effective weapons to weaken the Church - indulgence and endorsement. Diocletian is considered the worst emperor in Rome's history and the greatest antagonist of the Christian faith. He led a violent attempt to destroy the Bible from the face of the earth. Under his leadership many Roman cities held public burnings of the sacred Scriptures. During the second and third centuries this persecution age saw hundreds of Christians brought into the amphitheater of Rome to be fed to angry lions while thousands of spectators cheered. Many were crucified; others were covered with animal skins and tortured to death by wild dogs. There were some covered in tar and set on fire to serve as torches. They were boiled in oil and burned at the stake, as was Polycarp in the city of Smyrna itself in A.D. 156. One church historian has estimated that during this period, nearly five MILLION Christians were martyred for the testimony of the Lord Jesus Christ.
>
> A Thriving Church
>
> Evidence of the Supernatural nature of the Church can be seen in the fact the Church reached its greatest numbers in proportion to world population during this time of persecution. In addition to the establishment of churches in many parts of the world, this Church age distinguished itself by its production of many hand-copied Scriptures and manuscripts of the sacred Scriptures and the translation of

Scripture into many languages. Early in this period the Bible was translated into Syriac, in which is known as the Peshito manuscripts, which became the official Scriptures of the Eastern churches and from which translations were made into Arabic, Persian, and Armenian. In the second century the Bible was translated into Latin in what is called the Old Latin Version. This has become the Bible of the Western churches and has been translated into numerous other languages.[6]

The Second Church Age

For: *"I know your works, oppression, and your poverty (but you are rich), and the blasphemy of those who say they are Jews, and they are not, but are a synagogue of Satan."*

Against/warning: *"Don't be afraid of the things which you are about to suffer. Behold, the devil is about to throw some of you into prison, that you may be tested; and you will have oppression for ten days. Be faithful to death"*

The Double-edged sword:

Words that give life: *". . . I will give you the crown of life. He who has an ear, let him hear what the Spirit says to the assemblies. He who overcomes won't be harmed by the second death."*

The words that give judgment: None

The characteristics of His person to this church: *"The first and the last, who was dead, and has come to life says these things"*

In the last church who is a materially rich church, Jesus tells them they are spiritually poor. To this materially poor and persecuted church He tells them they are rich spiritually. However, this is a rich city of trade at its time. It seems their own people (non-believing Jews) are the ones who slander them and incite the government against them. Jesus is telling them to die physically will win them eternal life. They will not have to suffer a worse death, (death after the last day of judgment), the second death. He also gives His personal qualifications for having the right to not only say these things, but to ask of them to go through this tribulation in order to be purified.

"These are the words of him who is the First and the Last, <u>who died and came to life again."</u> By saying this about Himself, Jesus is saying: 1) I would never ask you to do something I have not already done. 2) It will be alright, behold they killed Me, yet I am alive, so it will be with you . . . because I live, you also will live.

NIV Jn 14:19 . . . Because I live, you also will live.
NIV Jn 14:20 On that day you will realize that I am in my Father, and you are in me, and I am in you.

It is also noteworthy that in the article quoted above it is said:

> "Evidence of the Supernatural nature of the Church can be seen in the fact the Church reached its greatest numbers in proportion to world population during this time of persecution. In addition to the establishment of churches in many parts of the world, this church age distinguished itself. . ."

It is through the suffering of tribulations Jesus populates heaven. It is through their holding dearer to their hearts their love for Jesus more than their own lives (along with the rejection and hatred that the world has for them) that Jesus can detach His *Church Corrupt* from their integration into the world. What makes the quote above noteworthy is that we see through the suffering and loss of life of this church in this city that it is true: Jesus can increase His Kingdom by using the pursuits of evil in others.

As pointed out the true tenness of the words of Jesus and the persecution of the Church does not have its fullness until the end. This will be when the world is divided into ten monarchs under the beast and the great tribulation begins—a worldwide hunt to imprison and kill all the people of God. What this helps us understand is that it is true that Jesus is not only talking to the church of Smyrna directly, but He is also speaking to the entire Church, whose persecution climaxes when it reaches the very end of the entire Church Age. In addition, although this letter is addressed to the church of Smyrna, listen to what Jesus says in verse 11 (below):

Rev 2:11 *"Anyone who is willing to hear should listen to the Spirit and* understand what the Spirit is saying to the churches.

Jesus is talking to the entire Church for its entire Age from beginning to end. What He says is prophetic not only to the church of Smyrna who He is informing of things to come, but to all of His Church which will suffer the global tenness of the ten horns or kings of the beast during the great tribulation.

Another clue that tells us this is true; Jesus says to this church that the people who will be persecuted will not be harmed by the second death. This is brought up one other time in Revelation. It concerns those who are part of the first resurrection.

WEB Rev 20:6 *Blessed and holy is he who has part in the first resurrection. Over these, the second death has no power, but they will be priests of God and of Christ, and will reign with him one thousand years.*

What makes this interesting is the only ones who take part in the first resurrection are those who endured the persecution of the beast during the time of the great tribulation. The martyrs of the church of Smyrna will not participate in the first resurrection. They already have their celestial bodies long before the event of the first resurrection comes.

Note: All who have died or were raptured before the great tribulation instantly received their celestial bodies. Not only did they not experience death but have avoided the second death on the last day of judgment. We will see how this is true later in this study. However, for now we wanted to use this reference of the second death to show how Jesus was not just talking to the church in Smyrna, but to the entire seven Church ages which end with the great tribulation.

Because of the use of ten it helps pinpoint the exact time of the second Church age. The second Church age started with the first of the ten Roman emperors who persecuted the Christians (Nero 64 AD). The second Church age ends with the tenth emperor who persecuted the Christians for a ten year time period

(Diocletian 303 AD-313 AD). After that time period the next Roman emperor is Constantine. With him the persecution not only ends, but the Church in the Roman Empire enjoys a status of privilege.

The tenness of persecution Jesus spoke of did not begin with Smyrna. Nor did it end with them and the second Church age. However, the church of Smyrna did suffer ten years of persecution under the tenth monarch of the Roman Empire who persecuted Christians. The church of Smyrna was the local and contemporary expression of the tenness of suffering which continues in pockets around the world. Suffering after the second Church age continues and will accumulate growing in scope until the global and end times expression completes the tenness of persecution of the Christians with the ten kings (or horns) of the beast.

The local and contemporary expression had ten (for the most part) succeeding kings of the Roman Empire persecute the Christians. Jesus referred to that as "ten days," meaning a day equals the reign of one of the ten emperors of the Roman Empire who persecuted the Christians. This totaled in ten reigns of ten different emperors, or ten days (as Jesus calls them) until the end of persecution (in the Roman Empire) finally came through Constantine. Those ten monarchs and their reigns are the second Church age.

Now this is more evidence that Jesus was not just writing this letter to the church of Smyrna. He tells them that, "you will have oppression for ten days." We understand that when Jesus says a "day" He means an entire reign of a monarch/king. Therefore, the first day or monarch and his Reign was Nero in 64 AD. However, Smyrna's time of persecution was not until the tenth day or the tenth monarch during his reign beginning (the persecution) in 303 AD for ten years. Yet Jesus said in His letter to this church "you" will have oppression for ten days. By using the word "you" describing something occurring in scope before and after the church addressed, tells us clearly that He is talking to all of His Church for the entire Church Age and not to the specific church addressed.

The global and end times expression will have ten simultaneous kings who together rule all the nations of the earth and persecute the Christians. There will be no place to hide. The tenness of God's plan of salvation will not be complete until the ten horns of the beast come into power and persecute the worldwide Church. Jesus knew this when He wrote this letter to the church of Smyrna and had it in mind when He told them they will be persecuted for ten days.

Note: The first Church age begins with the Day of Pentecost in 33 AD until 64 AD lasting 31 years. The second Church age begins when Nero was emperor. When in 64 AD he broke out against the Christians in Rome, blaming them for the fire which burned down Rome. The second Church age ends with Diocletian in 313 AD. The second Church age lasted 249 years. The third Church age begins when the emperor Constantine made the Edict of Milan which legalized the practice of the Christian religion. It took away the death sentence for practicing Christianity and thereby ended the ten year period of persecution imposed by Diocletian against Christians in the Roman Empire.

Note of interest: John wrote the book of Revelation during the second Church age in 96 AD.

Here is an excerpt from chapter 2 of Foxe's Book of Martyrs describing the ten days or monarchs of persecution and their emperors:

The First Persecution, Under Nero, A.D. 67

The first persecution of the Church took place in the year 67, under Nero, the sixth emperor of Rome. This monarch reigned for the space of five years, with tolerable credit to himself, but then gave way to the greatest extravagancy of temper, and to the most atrocious barbarities. Among other diabolical whims, he ordered that the city of Rome should be set on fire, which order was executed by his officers, guards, and servants. While the imperial city was in flames, he went up to the tower of Macaenas, played upon his harp, sung the song of the burning of Troy, and openly declared that 'he wished the ruin of all things before his death.' Besides the noble pile, called the Circus, many other palaces and houses were consumed; several thousands perished in the flames, were smothered in the smoke, or buried beneath the ruins.

This dreadful conflagration continued nine days; when Nero, finding that his conduct was greatly blamed, and a severe odium cast upon him, determined to lay the whole upon the Christians, at once to excuse himself, and have an opportunity of glutting his sight with new cruelties. This was the occasion of the first persecution; and the barbarities exercised on the Christians were such as even excited the commiseration of the Romans themselves. Nero even refined upon cruelty, and contrived all manner of punishments for the Christians that the most infernal imagination could design. In particular, he had some sewed up in skins of wild beasts, and then worried by dogs until they expired; and others dressed in shirts made stiff with wax, fixed to axletrees, and set on fire in his gardens, in order to illuminate them. This persecution was general throughout the whole Roman Empire; but it rather increased than diminished the spirit of Christianity. In the course of it, St. Paul and St. Peter were martyred.

To their names may be added, Erastus, chamberlain of Corinth; Aristarchus, the Macedonian, and Trophimus, an Ephesians, converted by St. Paul, and fellow-laborer with him, Joseph, commonly called Barsabas, and Ananias, bishop of Damascus; each of the Seventy.

The Second Persecution, Under Domitian, A.D. 81

The emperor Domitian, who was naturally inclined to cruelty, first slew his brother, and then raised the second persecution against the Christians. In his rage he put to death some of the Roman senators, some through malice; and others to confiscate their estates. He then commanded all the lineage of David be put to death.

Among the numerous martyrs that suffered during this persecution was Simeon, bishop of Jerusalem, who was crucified; and St. John, who was boiled in oil, and afterward banished to Patmos. Flavia, the daughter of a Roman senator, was likewise banished to Pontus; and a law was made, "That no Christian, once brought before the tribunal, should be exempted from punishment without renouncing his religion."

A variety of fabricated tales were, during this reign, composed in order to injure the Christians. Such was the infatuation of the pagans, that, if famine, pestilence, or earthquakes afflicted any of the Roman provinces, it was laid upon the Christians. These persecutions among the Christians increased the number of informers and many, for the sake of gain, swore away the lives of the innocent.

Another hardship was, that, when any Christians were brought before the magistrates, a test oath was proposed, when, if they refused to take it, death was pronounced against them; and if they confessed themselves Christians, the sentence was the same.

The following were the most remarkable among the numerous martyrs who suffered during this persecution.

Dionysius, the Areopagite, was an Athenian by birth, and educated in all the useful and ornamental literature of Greece. He then travelled to Egypt to study astronomy, and made very particular observations on the great and supernatural eclipse, which happened at the time of our Savior's crucifixion.

The sanctity of his conversation and the purity of his manners recommended him so strongly to the Christians in general, that he was appointed bishop of Athens.

Nicodemus, a benevolent Christian of some distinction, suffered at Rome during the rage of Domitian's persecution.

Protasius and Gervasius were martyred at Milan.

Timothy was the celebrated disciple of St. Paul, and bishop of Ephesus, where he zealously governed the Church until A.D. 97. At this period, as the pagans were about to celebrate a feast called Catagogion, Timothy, meeting the procession, severely reproved them for their ridiculous idolatry, which so exasperated the people that they fell upon him with their clubs, and beat him in so dreadful a manner that he expired of the bruises two days later.

The Third Persecution, Under Trajan, A.D. 108

In the third persecution Pliny the Second, a man learned and famous, seeing the lamentable slaughter of Christians, and moved therewith to pity, wrote to Trajan, certifying him that there were many thousands of them daily put to death, of which none did any thing contrary to the Roman laws worthy of persecution. "The whole account they gave of their crime or error (whichever it is to be called) amounted only to this--viz. that they were accustomed on a stated day to meet before daylight, and to repeat together a set form of prayer to Christ as a God, and to bind themselves by an obligation--not indeed to commit wickedness; but, on the contrary--never to commit theft, robbery, or adultery, never to falsify their word, never to defraud any man: after which it was their custom to separate, and reassemble to partake in common of a harmless meal."

In this persecution suffered the blessed martyr, Ignatius, who is held in famous reverence among very many. This Ignatius was appointed to the bishopric of Antioch next after Peter in succession. Some do say, that he, being sent from Syria to Rome, because he professed Christ, was given to the wild beasts to be devoured. It is also said of him, that when he passed through Asia, being under the most strict custody of his keepers, he strengthened and confirmed the churches through all the cities as he went, both with his exhortations and preaching of the Word of God. Accordingly, having come to Smyrna, he wrote to the Church at Rome, exhorting them not to use means for his deliverance from martyrdom, lest they should deprive him of that which he most longed and hoped for. "Now I begin to be a disciple. I care for nothing, of visible or invisible things, so that I may but win Christ. Let fire and the cross, let the companies of wild beasts, let breaking of bones and tearing of limbs, let the grinding of the whole body, and all the malice of the devil, come upon me; be it so, only may I win Christ Jesus!" And even when he was sentenced to be thrown to the beasts, such as the burning desire that he had to suffer, that he spake, what time he heard the lions roaring, saying: "I am the wheat of Christ: I am going to be ground with the teeth of wild beasts, that I may be found pure bread."

Trajan being succeeded by Adrian, the latter continued this third persecution with as much severity as his predecessor. About this time Alexander, bishop of Rome, with his two deacons, were martyred; as were Quirinus and Hernes, with their families; Zenon, a Roman nobleman, and about ten thousand other Christians.

In Mount Ararat many were crucified, crowned with thorns, and spears run into their sides, in imitation of Christ's passion. Eustachius, a brave and successful Roman commander, was by the emperor ordered to join in an idolatrous sacrifice to celebrate some of his own victories; but his faith (being a Christian in his heart) was so much greater than his vanity, that he nobly refused it. Enraged at the denial, the ungrateful emperor forgot the service of this skilful commander, and ordered him and his whole family to be martyred.

At the martyrdom of Faustines and Jovita, brothers and citizens of Brescia, their torments were so many, and their patience so great, that Calocerius, a pagan, beholding them, was struck with admiration, and exclaimed in a kind of ecstasy, "Great is the God of the Christians!" for which he was apprehended, and suffered a similar fate.

Many other similar cruelties and rigors were exercised against the Christians, until Quadratus, bishop of Athens, made a learned apology in their favor before the emperor, who happened to be there and Aristides, a philosopher of the same city, wrote an elegant epistle, which caused Adrian to relax in his severities, and relent in their favor.

Adrian dying A.D. 138, was succeeded by Antoninus Pius, one of the most amiable monarchs that ever reigned, and who stayed the persecutions against the Christians.

The Fourth Persecution, Under Marcus Aurelius Antoninus, A.D. 162

Marcus Aurelius, followed about the year of our Lord 161, a man of nature more stern and severe; and, although in study of philosophy and in civil government no less commendable, yet, toward the Christians sharp and fierce; by whom was moved the fourth persecution.

The cruelties used in this persecution were such that many of the spectators shuddered with horror at the sight, and were astonished at the intrepidity of the sufferers. Some of the martyrs were obliged to pass, with their already wounded feet, over thorns, nails, sharp shells, etc. upon their points, others were scourged until their sinews and veins lay bare, and after suffering the most excruciating tortures that could be devised, they were destroyed by the most terrible deaths.

Germanicus, a young man, but a true Christian, being delivered to the wild beasts on account of his faith, behaved with such astonishing courage that several pagans became converts to a faith which inspired such fortitude.

Polycarp, the venerable bishop of Smyrna, hearing that persons were seeking for him, escaped, but was discovered by a child. After feasting the guards who apprehended him, he desired an hour in prayer, which being allowed, he prayed with such fervency, that his guards repented that they had been instrumental in taking him. He was, however, carried before the proconsul, condemned, and burnt in the market place.

The proconsul then urged him, saying, "Swear, and I will release thee;--reproach Christ."

Polycarp answered, "Eighty and six years have I served him, and he never once wronged me; how then shall I blaspheme my King, Who hath saved me?" At the stake to which he was only tied, but not nailed as usual, as he assured them he should stand immovable, the flames, on their kindling the fagots, encircled his body, like an arch, without touching him; and the executioner, on seeing this, was ordered to pierce him with a sword, when so great a quantity of blood flowed out as extinguished the fire. But his body, at the instigation of the enemies of the Gospel, especially Jews, was ordered to be consumed in the pile, and the request of his friends, who wished to give it Christian burial, rejected. They nevertheless collected his bones and as much of his remains as possible, and caused them to be decently interred.

Metrodorus, a minister, who preached boldly, and Pionius, who made some excellent apologies for the Christian faith, were likewise burnt. Carpus and Papilus, two worthy Christians, and Agatonica, a pious woman, suffered martyrdom at Pergamopolis, in Asia.

Felicitatis, an illustrious Roman lady, of a considerable family, and the most shining virtues, was a devout Christian. She had seven sons, whom she had educated with the most exemplary piety.

Januarius, the eldest, was scourged, and pressed to death with weights; Felix and Philip, the two next had their brains dashed out with clubs; Silvanus, the fourth, was murdered by being thrown from a precipice; and the three younger sons, Alexander, Vitalis, and Martial, were beheaded. The mother was beheaded with the same sword as the three latter.

Justin, the celebrated philosopher, fell a martyr in this persecution. He was a native of Neapolis, in Samaria, and was born A.D. 103. Justin was a great lover of truth, and a universal scholar; he investigated the Stoic and Peripatetic philosophy, and attempted the Pythagorean; but the behavior of our of its professors disgusting him, he applied himself to the Platonic, in which he took great delight. About the year 133, when he was thirty years of age, he became a convert to Christianity, and then, for the first time, perceived the real nature of truth.

He wrote an elegant epistle to the Gentiles, and employed his talents in convincing the Jews of the truth of the Christian rites; spending a great deal of time in travelling, until he took up his abode in Rome, and fixed his habitation upon the Viminal mount.

He kept a public school, taught many who afterward became great men, and wrote a treatise to confuse heresies of all kinds. As the pagans began to treat the Christians with great severity, Justin wrote his first apology in their favor. This piece displays great learning and genius, and occasioned the emperor to publish an edict in favor of the Christians.

Soon after, he entered into frequent contests with Crescens, a person of a vicious life and conversation, but a celebrated cynic philosopher; and his arguments appeared so powerful, yet disgusting to the cynic, that he resolved on, and in the sequel accomplished, his destruction.

The second apology of Justin, upon certain severities, gave Crescens the cynic an opportunity of prejudicing the emperor against the writer of it; upon which Justin, and six of his companions, were apprehended. Being commanded to sacrifice to the pagan idols, they refused, and were condemned to be scourged, and then beheaded; which sentence was executed with all imaginable severity.

Several were beheaded for refusing to sacrifice to the image of Jupiter; in particular Concordus, a deacon of the city of Spolito.

Some of the restless northern nations having risen in arms against Rome, the emperor marched to encounter them. He was, however, drawn into an ambuscade, and dreaded the loss of his whole army. Enveloped with mountains, surrounded by enemies, and perishing with thirst, the pagan deities were invoked in vain; when the men belonging to the militine, or thundering legion, who were all Christians, were commanded to call upon their God for succor. A miraculous deliverance immediately ensued; a prodigious quantity of rain fell, which, being caught by the men, and filling their dykes, afforded a sudden and astonishing relief. It appears that the storm which miraculously flashed in the face of the enemy so intimidated them, that part deserted to the Roman army; the rest were defeated, and the revolted provinces entirely recovered.

This affair occasioned the persecution to subside for some time, at least in those parts immediately under the inspection of the emperor; but we find that it soon after raged in France, particularly at Lyons, where the tortures to which many of the Christians were put, almost exceed the powers of description.

The principal of these martyrs were Vetius Agathus, a young man; Blandina, a Christian lady, of a weak constitution; Sanctus, a deacon of Vienna; red hot plates of brass were placed upon the tenderest parts of his body; Biblias, a weak woman, once an apostate. Attalus, of Pergamus; and Pothinus, the venerable bishop of Lyons, who was ninety years of age. Blandina, on the day when she and the three other champions were first brought into the amphitheater, she was suspended on a piece of wood fixed in the ground, and exposed as food for the wild beasts; at which time, by her earnest prayers, she encouraged others. But none of the wild beasts would touch her, so that she was remanded to prison. When she was again produced for the third and last time, she was accompanied by Ponticus, a youth of fifteen, and the constancy of their faith so enraged the multitude that neither the sex of the one nor the youth of the other were respected, being exposed to all manner of punishments and tortures. Being strengthened by Blandina, he persevered unto death; and she, after enduring all the torments heretofore mentioned, was at length slain with the sword.

When the Christians, upon these occasions, received martyrdom, they were ornamented, and crowned with garlands of flowers; for which they, in heaven, received eternal crowns of glory.

It has been said that the lives of the early Christians consisted of "persecution above ground and prayer below ground." Their lives are expressed by the Coliseum and the catacombs. Beneath Rome are the excavations which we call the catacombs, which were at once temples and tombs. The early Church of Rome might well be called the Church of the Catacombs. There are some sixty catacombs near Rome, in which some six hundred miles of galleries have been traced, and these are not all. These galleries are about eight feet high and from three to five feet wide, containing on either side several rows of long, low, horizontal recesses, one above another like berths in a ship. In these the dead bodies were placed and the front closed, either by a single marble slab or several great tiles laid in mortar. On these slabs or tiles, epitaphs or symbols are graved or painted. Both pagans and Christians buried their dead in these catacombs. When the Christian graves have been opened the skeletons tell their own terrible tale. Heads are found severed from the body, ribs and shoulder blades are broken, bones are often calcined from fire. But despite the awful story of persecution that we may read here, the inscriptions breathe forth peace and joy and triumph. Here are a few:

"Here lies Marcia, put to rest in a dream of peace."

"Lawrence to his sweetest son, borne away of angels."

"Victorious in peace and in Christ."

"Being called away, he went in peace."

Remember when reading these inscriptions the story the skeletons tell of persecution, of torture, and of fire.

But the full force of these epitaphs is seen when we <u>contrast them with the pagan epitaphs, such as</u>:

"Live for the present hour, since we are sure of nothing else."

"I lift my hands against the gods who took me away at the age of twenty though I had done no harm."

"Once I was not. Now I am not. I know nothing about it, and it is no concern of mine."

"Traveler, curse me not as you pass, for I am in darkness and cannot answer."

The most frequent Christian symbols on the walls of the catacombs, are, the good shepherd with the lamb on his shoulder, a ship under full sail, harps, anchors, crowns, vines, and above all the fish.

The Fifth Persecution, Commencing with Severus, A.D. 192

Severus, having been recovered from a severe fit of sickness by a Christian, became a great favorer of the Christians in general; but the prejudice and fury of the ignorant multitude prevailing, obsolete laws were put in execution against the Christians. The progress of Christianity alarmed the pagans, and they revived the stale calumny of placing accidental misfortunes to the account of its professors, A.D. 192.

But, though persecuting malice raged, yet the Gospel shone with resplendent brightness; and, firm as an impregnable rock, withstood the attacks of its boisterous enemies with success. Tertullian, who lived in this age, informs us that if the Christians had collectively withdrawn themselves from the Roman territories, the empire would have been greatly depopulated.

Victor, bishop of Rome, suffered martyrdom in the first year of the third century, A.D. 201. Leonidus, the father of the celebrated Origen, was beheaded for being a Christian. Many of Origen's hearers likewise suffered martyrdom; particularly two brothers, named Plutarchus and Serenus; another Serenus, Heron, and Heraclides, were beheaded. Rhais had boiled pitch poured upon her head, and was then burnt, as was Marcella her mother. Potainiena, the sister of Rhais, was executed in the same manner as Rhais had been; but Basilides, an officer belonging to the army, and ordered to attend her execution, became her convert.

Basilides being, as an officer, required to take a certain oath, refused, saying, that he could not swear by the Roman idols, as he was a Christian. Struck with surpsie, the people could not, at first, believe what they heard; but he had no sooner confirmed the same, than he was dragged before the judge, committed to prison, and speedily afterward beheaded.

Irenaeus, bishop of Lyons, was born in Greece, and received both a polite and a Christian education. It is generally supposed that the account of the persecutions at Lyons was written by himself. He succeeded the martyr Pothinus as bishop of Lyons, and ruled his diocese with great propriety; he was a zealous opposer of heresies in general, and, about A.D. 187, he wrote a celebrated tract against heresy. Victor, the bishop of Rome, wanting to impose the keeping of Easter there, in preference to other places, it occasioned some disorders among the Christians. In particular, Irenaeus wrote him a synodical epistle, in the name of the Gallic churches. This zeal, in favor of Christianity, pointed him out as an object of resentment to the emperor; and in A.D. 202, he was beheaded.

The persecutions now extending to Africa, many were martyred in that quarter of the globe; the most particular of whom we shall mention.

Perpetua, a married lady, of about twenty-two years. Those who suffered with her were, Felicitas, a married lady, big with child at the time of her being apprehended, and Revocatus, catechumen of Carthage, and a slave. The names of the other prisoners, destined to suffer upon this occasion, were Saturninus, Secundulus, and Satur. On the day appointed for their execution, they were led to the amphitheater. Satur, Saturninus, and Revocatus were ordered to run the gauntlet between the hunters, or such as had the care of the wild beasts. The hunters being drawn up in two ranks, they ran between, and were severely lashed as they passed. Felicitas and Perpetua were stripped, in order to be thrown to a mad bull, which made his first attack upon Perpetua, and stunned her; he then darted at Felicitas, and gored her dreadfully; but not killing them, the executioner did that office with a sword. Revocatus and Satur were destroyed by wild beasts; Saturninus was beheaded; and Secundulus died in prison. These executions were in the 205, on the eighth day of March.

Speratus and twelve others were likewise beheaded; as was Andocles in France. Asclepiades, bishop of Antioch, suffered many tortures, but his life was spared.

Cecilia, a young lady of good family in Rome, was married to a gentleman named Valerian. She converted her husband and brother, who were beheaded; and the maximus, or officer, who led them to execution, becoming their convert, suffered the same fate. The lady was placed naked in a scalding bath, and having continued there a considerable time, her head was struck off with a sword, A.D. 222.

Calistus, bishop of Rome, was martyred, A.D. 224; but the manner of his death is not recorded; and Urban, bishop of Rome, met the same fate A.D. 232.

The Sixth Persecution, Under Maximus, A.D. 235

A.D. 235, was in the time of Maximinus. In Cappadocia, the president, Seremianus, did all he could to exterminate the Christians from that province.

The principal persons who perished under this reign were Pontianus, bishop of Rome; Anteros, a Grecian, his successor, who gave offence to the government by collecting the acts of the martyrs, Pammachius and Quiritus, Roman senators, with all their families, and many other Christians; Simplicius, senator; Calepodius, a Christian minister, thrown into the Tyber; Martina, a noble and beautiful virgin; and Hippolitus, a Christian prelate, tied to a wild horse, and dragged until he expired.

During this persecution, raised by Maximinus, numberless Christians were slain without trial, and buried indiscriminately in heaps, sometimes fifty or sixty being cast into a pit together, without the least decency.

The tyrant Maximinus dying, A.D. 238, was succeeded by Gordian, during whose reign, and that of his successor Philip, the Church was free from persecution for the space of more than ten years; but in A.D. 249, a violent persecution broke out in Alexandria, at the instigation of a pagan priest, without the knowledge of the emperor.

The Seventh Persecution, Under Decius, A.D. 249

This was occasioned partly by the hatred he bore to his predecessor Philip, who was deemed a Christian and was partly by his jealousy concerning the amazing increase of Christianity; for the heathen temples began to be forsaken, and the Christian churches thronged.

These reasons stimulated Decius to attempt the very extirpation of the name of Christian; and it was unfortunate for the Gospel, that many errors had, about this time, crept into the Church: the Christians were at variance with each other; self-interest divided those whom social love ought to have united; and the virulence of pride occasioned a variety of factions.

The heathens in general were ambitious to enforce the imperial decrees upon this occasion, and looked upon the murder of a Christian as a merit to themselves. The martyrs, upon this occasion, were innumerable; but the principal we shall give some account of.

Fabian, the bishop of Rome, was the first person of eminence who felt the severity of this persecution. The deceased emperor, Philip, had, on account of his integrity, committed his treasure to the care of this good man. But Decius, not finding as much as his avarice made him expect, determined to wreak his vengeance on the good prelate. He was accordingly seized; and on January 20, A.D. 250, he suffered decapitation.

Julian, a native of Cilicia, as we are informed by St. Chrysostom, was seized upon for being a Christian. He was put into a leather bag, together with a number of serpents and scorpions, and in that condition thrown into the sea.

Peter, a young man, amiable for the superior qualities of his body and mind, was beheaded for refusing to sacrifice to Venus. He said, "I am astonished you should sacrifice to an infamous woman, whose debaucheries even your own historians record, and whose life consisted of such actions as your laws would punish. No, I shall offer the true God the acceptable sacrifice of praises and prayers." Optimus, the proconsul of Asia, on hearing this, ordered the prisoner to be stretched upon a wheel, by which all his bones were broken, and then he was sent to be beheaded.

Nichomachus, being brought before the proconsul as a Christian, was ordered to sacrifice to the pagan idols. Nichomachus replied, "I cannot pay that respect to devils, which is only due to the Almighty." This speech so much enraged the proconsul that Nichomachus was put to the rack. After enduring the torments for a time, he recanted; but scarcely had he given this proof of his frailty, than he fell into the greatest agonies, dropped down on the ground, and expired immediately.

Denisa, a young woman of only sixteen years of age, who beheld this terrible judgment, suddenly exclaimed, "O unhappy wretch, why would you buy a moment's ease at the expense of a miserable eternity!" Optimus, hearing this, called to her, and Denisa avowing herself to be a Christian, she was beheaded, by his order, soon after.

Andrew and Paul, two companions of Nichomachus, the martyr, A.D. 251, suffered martyrdom by stoning, and expired, calling on their blessed Redeemer.

Alexander and Epimachus, of Alexandria, were apprehended for being Christians: and, confessing the accusation, were beat with staves, torn with hooks, and at length burnt in the fire; and we are informed, in a fragment preserved by Eusebius, that four female martyrs suffered on the same day, and at the same place, but not in the same manner; for these were beheaded.

Lucian and Marcian, two wicked pagans, though skilful magicians, becoming converts to Christianity, to make amends for their former errors, lived the lives of hermits, and subsisted upon bread and water only. After some time spent in this manner, they became zealous preachers, and made many converts. The persecution, however, raging at this time, they were seized upon, and carried before Sabinus, the governor of Bithynia. On being asked by what authority they took upon themselves to preach, Lucian answered, 'That the laws of charity and humanity obliged all men to endeavor the conversion of their neighbors, and to do everything in their power to rescue them from the snares of the devil.'

Lucian having answered in this manner, Marcian said, "Their conversion was by the same grace which was given to St. Paul, who, from a zealous persecutor of the Church, became a preacher of the Gospel."

The proconsul, finding that he could not prevail with them to renounce their faith, condemned them to be burnt alive, which sentence was soon after executed.

Trypho and Respicius, two eminent men, were seized as Christians, and imprisoned at Nice. Their feet were pierced with nails; they were dragged through the streets, scourged, torn with iron hooks, scorched with lighted torches, and at length beheaded, February 1, A.D. 251.

Agatha, a Sicilian lady, was not more remarkable for her personal and acquired endowments, than her piety; her beauty was such, that Quintian, governor of Sicily, became enamored of her, and made many attempts upon her chastity without success. In order to gratify his passions with the greater conveniency, he put the virtuous lady into the hands of Aphrodica, a very infamous and licentious woman. This wretch tried every artifice to win her to the desired prostitution; but found all her efforts were vain; for her chastity was impregnable, and she well knew that virtue alone could procure true happiness. Aphrodica acquainted Quintian with the inefficacy of her endeavors, who, enaged to be foiled in his designs, changed his lust into resentment. On her confessing that she was a Christian, he determined to gratify his revenge, as he could not his passion. Pursuant to his orders, she was scourged, burnt with red-hot irons, and torn with sharp hooks. Having borne these torments with admirable fortitude, she was next laid naked upon live coals, intermingled with glass, and then being carried back to prison, she there expired on February 5, 251.

Cyril, bishop of Gortyna, was seized by order of Lucius, the governor of that place, who, nevertheless, exhorted him to obey the imperial mandate, perform the sacrifices, and save his venerable person from destruction; for he was now eighty-four years of age. The good prelate replied that as he had long taught others to save their souls, he should only think now of his own salvation. The worthy prelate heard his fiery sentence without emotion, walked cheerfully to the place of execution, and underwent his martyrdom with great fortitude.

The persecution raged in no place more than the Island of Crete; for the governor, being exceedingly active in executing the imperial decrees, that place streamed with pious blood.

Babylas, a Christian of a liberal education, became bishop of Antioch, A.D. 237, on the demise of Zebinus. He acted with inimitable zeal, and governed the Church with admirable prudence during the most tempestuous times.

The first misfortune that happened to Antioch during his mission, was the siege of it by Sapor, king of Persia; who, having overrun all Syria, took and plundered this city among others, and used the Christian inhabitants with greater severity than the rest, but was soon totally defeated by Gordian.

After Gordian's death, in the reign of Decius, that emperor came to Antioch, where, having a desire to visit an assembly of Christians, Babylas opposed him, and absolutely refused to let him come in. The emperor dissembled his anger at that time; but soon sending for the bishop, he sharply reproved him for his insolence, and then ordered him to sacrifice to the pagan deities as an expiation for his ofence. This being refused, he was committed to prison, loaded with chains, treated with great severities, and then beheaded, together with three young men who had been his pupils. A.D. 251.

Alexander, bishop of Jerusalem, about this time was cast into prison on account of his religion, where he died through the severity of his confinement.

Julianus, an old man, lame with the gout, and Cronion, another Christian, were bound on the backs of camels, severely scourged, and then thrown into a fire and consumed. Also forty virgins, at Antioch, after being imprisoned, and scourged, were burnt.

In the year of our Lord 251, the emperor Decius having erected a pagan temple at Ephesus, he commanded all who were in that city to sacrifice to the idols. This order was nobly refused by seven of his own soldiers, viz. Maximianus, Martianus, Joannes, Malchus, Dionysius, Seraion, and Constantinus. The emperor wishing to win these soldiers to renounce their faith by his entreaties and lenity, gave them a considerable respite until he returned from an expedition. During the emperor's absence, they escaped, and hid themselves in a cavern; which the emperor being informed of at his return, the mouth of the cave was closed up, and they all perished with hunger.

Theodora, a beautiful young lady of Antioch, on refusing to sacrifice to the Roman idols, was condemned to the stews, that her virtue might be sacrificed to the brutality of lust. Didymus, a Christian, disguised himself in the habit of a Roman soldier, went to the house, informed Theodora who he was, and advised her to make her escape in his clothes. This being effected, and a man found in the brothel instead of a beautiful lady, Didymus was taken before the president, to whom confessing the truth, and owning that he was a Christian the sentence of death was immediately pronounced against him. Theodora, hearing that her deliverer was likely to suffer, came to the judge, threw herself at his feet, and begged that the sentence might fall on her as the guilty person; but, deaf to the cries of the innocent, and insensible to the calls of justice, the inflexible judge condemned both; when they were executed accordingly, being first beheaded, and their bodies afterward burnt.

Secundianus, having been accused as a Christian, was conveyed to prison by some soldiers. On the way, Verianus and Marcellinus said, "Where are you carrying the innocent?" This interrogatory occasioned them to be seized, and all three, after having been tortured, were hanged and decapitated.

Origen, the celebrated presbyter and catechist of Alexandria, at the age of sixty-four, was seized, thrown into a loathsome prison, laden with fetters, his feet placed in the stocks, and his legs extended to the utmost for several successive days. He was threatened with fire, and tormented by every lingering means the most infernal imaginations could suggest. During this cruel temporizing, the emperor Decius died, and Gallus, who succeeded him, engaging in a war with the Goths, the Christians met with a respite. In this interim, Origen obtained his enlargement, and, retiring to Tyre, he there remained until his death, which happened when he was in the sixty-ninth year of his age.

Gallus, the emperor, having concluded his wars, a plague broke out in the empire: sacrifices to the pagan deities were ordered by the emperor, and persecutions spread from the interior to the extreme parts of the empire, and many fell martyrs to the impetuosity of the rabble, as well as the prejudice of the magistrates. Among these were Cornelius, the Christian bishop of Rome, and Lucius, his successor, in 253.

Most of the errors which crept into the Church at this time arose from placing human reason in competition with revelation; but the fallacy of such arguments being proved by the most able divines, the opinions they had created vanished away like the stars before the sun.

The Eighth Persecution, Under Valerian, A.D. 257

Began under Valerian, in the month of April, 257, and continued for three years and six months. The martyrs that fell in this persecution were innumerable, and their tortures and deaths as various and painful. The most eminent martyrs were the following, though neither rank, sex, nor age were regarded.

Rufina and Secunda were two beautiful and accomplished ladies, daughters of Asterius, a gentleman of eminence in Rome. Rufina, the elder, was designed in marriage for Armentarius, a young nobleman; Secunda, the younger, for Verinus, a person of rank and opulence. The suitors, at the time of the persecution's commencing, were both Christians; but when danger appeared, to save their fortunes, they renounced their faith. They took great pains to persuade the ladies to do the same, but, disappointed in their purpose, the lovers were base enough to inform against the ladies, who, being apprehended as Christians, were brought before Junius Donatus, governor of Rome, where, A.D. 257, they sealed their martyrdom with their blood.

Stephen, bishop of Rome, was beheaded in the same year, and about that time Saturninus, the pious orthodox bishop of Toulouse, refusing to sacrifice to idols, was treated with all the barbarous indignities imaginable, and fastened by the feet to the tail of a bull. Upon a signal given, the enraged animal was driven down the steps of the temple, by which the worthy martyr's brains were dashed out.

Sextus succeeded Stephen as bishop of Rome. He is supposed to have been a Greek by birth or by extraction, and had for some time served in the capacity of a deacon under Stephen. His great fidelity, singular wisdom, and uncommon courage distinguished him upon many occasions; and the happy conclusion of a controversy with some heretics is generally ascribed to his piety and prudence. In the year 258, Marcianus, who had the management of the Roman government, procured an order from the emperor Valerian, to put to death all the Christian clergy in Rome, and hence the bishop with six of his deacons, suffered martyrdom in 258.

Let us draw near to the fire of martyred Lawrence, that our cold hearts may be warmed thereby. The merciless tyrant, understanding him to be not only a minister of the sacraments, but a distributor also of the Church riches, promised to himself a double prey, by the apprehension of one soul. First, with the rake of avarice to scrape to himself the treasure of poor Christians; then with the fiery fork of tyranny, so to toss and turmoil them, that they should wax weary of their profession. With furious face and cruel countenance, the greedy wolf demanded where this Lawrence had bestowed the substance of the Church: who, craving three days' respite, promised to declare where the treasure might be had. In the meantime, he caused a good number of poor Christians to be congregated. So, when the day of his answer was come, the persecutor strictly charged him to stand to his promise. Then valiant Lawrence, stretching out his arms over the poor, said: "These are the precious treasure of the Church; these are the treasure indeed, in whom the faith of Christ reigneth, in whom Jesus Christ hath His mansion-place. What more precious jewels can Christ have, than those in whom He hath promised to dwell? For so it is written, 'I was an hungered, and ye gave me meat: I was thirsty, and ye gave me drink: I was a stranger, and ye took me in.' And again, 'Inasmuch as ye have done it unto one of the least of these my brethren, ye have done it unto me.' What greater riches can Christ our Master possess, than the poor people in whom He loveth to be seen?"

O, what tongue is able to express the fury and madness of the tyrant's heart! Now he stamped, he stared, he ramped, he fared as one out of his wits: his eyes like fire glowed, his mouth like a boar formed, his teeth like a hellhound grinned. Now, not a reasonable man, but a roaring lion, he might be called.

"Kindle the fire (he cried)--of wood make no spare. Hath this villain deluded the emperor? Away with him, away with him: whip him with scourges, jerk him with rods, buffet him with fists, brain him with clubs. Jesteth the traitor with the emperor? Pinch him with fiery tongs, gird him with burning plates, bring out the strongest chains, and the fire-forks, and the grated bed of iron: on the fire with it; bind the rebel hand and foot; and when the bed is fire-hot, on with him: roast him, broil him, toss him, turn him: on pain of our high displeasure do every man his office, O ye tormentors."

The word was no sooner spoken, but all was done. After many cruel handlings, this meek lamb was laid, I will not say on his fiery bed of iron, but on his soft bed of down. So mightily God wrought with his martyr Lawrence, so miraculously God tempered His element the fire; that it became not a bed of consuming pain, but a pallet of nourishing rest.

In Africa the persecution raged with peculiar violence; many thousands received the crown of martyrdom, among whom the following were the most distinguished characters:

Cyprian, bishop of Carthage, an eminent prelate, and a pious ornament of the Church. The brightness of his genius was tempered by the solidity of his judgment; and with all the accomplishments of the gentleman, he blended the virtues of a Christian. His doctrines were orthodox and pure; his language easy and elegant; and his manners graceful and winning: in fine, he was both the pious and polite preacher. In his youth he was educated in the principles of Gentilism, and having a considerable fortune, he lived in the very extravagance of splendor, and all the dignity of pomp.

About the year 246, Coecilius, a Christian minister of Carthage, became the happy instrument of Cyprian's conversion: on which account, and for the great love that he always afterward bore for the author of his conversion, he was termed Coecilius Cyprian. Previous to his baptism, he studied the Scriptures with care and being struck with the beauties of the truths they contained, he determined to practise the virtues therein recommended. Subsequent to his baptism, he sold his estate, distributed the money among the poor, dressed himself in plain attire, and commenced a life of austerity. He was soon after made a presbyter; and, being greatly admired for his virtues and works, on the death of Donatus, in A.D. 248, he was almost unanimously elected bishop of Carthage.

Cyprian's care not only extended over Carthage, but to Numidia and Mauritania. In all his transactions he took great care to ask the advice of his clergy, knowing that unanimity alone could be of service to the Church, this being one of his maxims, "That the bishop was in the church, and the church in the bishop; so that unity can only be preserved by a close connexion between the pastor and his flock."

In A.D. 250, Cyprian was publicly proscribed by the emperor Decius, under the appellation of Coecilius Cyprian, bishop of the Christrians; and the universal cry of the pagans was, "Cyprian to the lions, Cyprian to the beasts." The bishop, however, withdrew from the rage of the populace, and his effects were immediately confiscated. During his retirement, he wrote thirty pious and elegant letters to his flock; but several schisms that then crept into the Church, gave him great uneasiness. The rigor of the persecution abating, he returned to Carthage, and did everything in his power to expunge erroneous opinions. A terrible plague breaking out in Carthage, it was as usual, laid to the charge of the Christians; and the magistrates began to persecute accordingly, which occasioned an epistle from them to Cyprian, in answer to which he vindicates the cause of Christianity. A.D. 257,

Cyprian was brought before the proconsul Aspasius Paturnus, who exiled him to a little city on the Lybian sea. On the death of this proconsul, he returned to Carthage, but was soon after seized, and carried before the new governor, who condemned him to be beheaded; which sentence was executed on the fourteenth of September, A.D. 258.

The disciples of Cyprian, martyred in this persecution, were Lucius, Flavian, Victoricus, Remus, Montanus, Julian, Primelus, and Donatian.

At Utica, a most terrible tragedy was exhibited: three hundred Christians were, by the orders of the proconsul, placed round a burning limekiln. A pan of coals and incense being prepared, they were commanded either to sacrifice to Jupiter, or to be thrown into the kiln. Unanimously refusing, they bravely jumped into the pit, and were immediately suffocated.

Fructuosus, bishop of Tarragon, in Spain, and his two deacons, Augurius and Eulogius, were burnt for being Christians.

Alexander, Malchus, and Priscus, three Christians of Palestine, with a woman of the same place, voluntarily accused themselves of being Christians; on which account they were sentenced to be devoured by tigers, which sentence was executed accordingly.

Maxima, Donatilla, and Secunda, three virgins of Tuburga, had gall and vinegar given them to drink, were then severely scourged, tormented on a gibbet, rubbed with lime, scorched on a gridiron, worried by wild beasts, and at length beheaded.

It is here proper to take notice of the singular but miserable fate of the emperor Valerian, who had so long and so terribly persecuted the Christians. This tyrant, by a stretagem, was taken prisoner by Sapor, emperor of Persia, who carried him into his own country, and there treated him with the most unexampled indignity, making him kneel down as the meanest slave, and treading upon him as a footstool when he mounted his horse. After having kept him for the space of seven years in this abject state of slavery, he caused his eyes to be put out, though he was then eighty-three years of age. This not satiating his desire of revenge, he soon after ordered his body to be flayed alive, and rubbed with salt, under which torments he expired; and thus fell one of the most tyrannical emperors of Rome, and one of the greatest persecutors of the Christians.

A.D. 260, Gallienus, the son of Valerian, succeeded him, and during his reign (a few martyrs excepted) the Church enjoyed peace for some years.

The Ninth Persecution Under Aurelian, A.D. 274

The principal sufferers were: Felix, bishop of Rome. This prelate was advanced to the Roman see in 274. He was the first martyr to Aurelian's petulancy, being beheaded on the twenty- second of December, in the same year.

Agapetus, a young gentleman, who sold his estate, and gave the money to the poor, was seized as a Christian, tortured, and then beheaded at Praeneste, a city within a day's journey of Rome.

These are the only martyrs justify upon record during this reign, as it was soon put to a stop by the emperor's being murdered by his own domestics, at Byzantium.

Aurelian was succeeded by Tacitus, who was followed by Probus, as the latter was by Carus: this emperor being killed by a thunder storm, his sons, Carnious and Numerian, succeeded him, and during all these reigns the Church had peace.

Diocletian mounted the imperial throne, A.D. 284; at first he showed great favor to the Christians. In the year 286, he associated Maximian with him in the empire; and some Christians were put to death before any general persecution broke out. Among these were Felician and Primus, two brothers.

Marcus and Marcellianus were twins, natives of Rome, and of noble descent. Their parents were heathens, but the tutors, to whom the education of the children was intrusted, brought them up as Christians. Their constancy at length subdued those who wished them to become pagans, and their parents and whole family became converts to a faith they had before reprobated. They were martyred by being tied to posts, and having their feet pierced with nails. After remaining in this situation for a day and a night, their sufferings were put an end to by thrusting lances through their bodies.

Zoe, the wife of the jailer, who had the care of the before- mentioned martyrs, was also converted by them, and hung upon a tree, with a fire of straw lighted under her. When her body was taken down, it was thrown into a river, with a large stone tied to it, in order to sink it.

In the year of Christ 286, a most remarkable affair occurred; a legion of soldiers, consisting of six thousand six hundred and sixty-six men, contained none but Christians. This legion was called the Theban Legion, because the men had been raised in Thebias: they were quartered in the east until the emperor Maximian ordered them to march to Gaul, to assist him against the rebels of Burgundy. They passed the Alps into Gaul, under the command of Mauritius, Candidus, and Exupernis, their worthy commanders, and at length joined the emperor. Maximian, about this time, ordered a general sacrifice, at which the whole army was to assist; and likewise he commanded that they should take the oath of allegiance and swear, at the saame time, to assist in the extirpation of Christianity in Gaul. Alarmed at these orders, each individual of the Theban Legion absolutely refused either to sacrifice or take the oaths prescribed. This so greatly enraged Maximian, that he ordered the legion to be decimated, that is, every tenth man to be selected from the rest, and put to the sword. This bloody order having been put in execution, those who remained alive were still inflexible, when a second decimation took place, and every tenth man of those living was put to death. This second severity made no more impression than the first had done; the soldiers preserved their fortitude and their principles, but by the advice of their officers they drew up a loyal remonstrance to the emperor. This, it might have been presumed, would have softened the emperor, but it had a contrary effect: for, enraged at their perseverance and unanimity, he commanded that the whole legion should be put to death, which was accordingly executed by the other troops, who cut them to pieces with their swords, September 22, 286.

Alban, from whom St. Alban's, in Hertfordshire, received its name, was the first British martyr. Great Britain had received the Gospel of Christ from Lucius, the first Christian king, but did not suffer from the rage of persecution for many years after. He was originally a pagan, but converted by a Christian ecclesiastic, named Amphibalus, whom he sheltered on account of his religion. The enemies of Amphibalus, having intelligence of the place where he was secreted, came to the house of Alban; in order to facilitate his escape, when the soldiers came, he offered himself up as the person they were seeking for. The deceit being detected, the governor ordered him to be scourged, and then he was sentenced to be beheaded, June 22, A.D. 287.

The venerable Bede assures us, that, upon this occasion, the executioner suddenly became a convert to Christianity, and entreated permission to die for Alban, or with him. Obtaining the latter request, they were beheaded by a soldier, who voluntarily undertook the task of executioner. This happened on the twenty-second of June, A.D. 287, at Verulam, now St. Alban's, in Hertfordshire, where a magnificent church was erected to his memory about the time of Constantine the Great. The edifice, being destroyed in the Saxon wars, was rebuilt by Offa, king of Mercia, and a monastery erected adjoining to it, some remains of which are still visible, and the church is a noble Gothic structure.

Faith, a Christian female, of Acquitain, in France, was ordered to be broiled upon a gridiron, and then beheaded; A.D. 287.

Quintin was a Christian, and a native of Rome, but determined to attempt the propagation of the Gospel in Gaul, with one Lucian, they preached together in Amiens; after which Lucian went to Beaumaris, where he was martyred. Quintin remained in Picardy, and was very zealous in his ministry. Being seized upon as a Christian, he was stretched with pullies until his joints were dislocated; his body was then torn with wire scourges, and boiling oil and pitch poured on his naked flesh; lighted torches were applied to his sides and armpits; and after he had been thus tortured, he was remanded back to prison, and died of the barbarities he had suffered, October 31, A.D. 287. His body was sunk in the Somme.

The Tenth Persecution, Under Diocletian, A.D. 303

Under the Roman emperors, commonly called the Era of the Martyrs, was occasioned partly by the increasing number and luxury of the Christians, and the hatred of Galerius, the adopted son of Diocletian, who, being stimulated by his mother, a bigoted pagan, never ceased persuading the emperor to enter upon the persecution, until he had accomplished his purpose.

The fatal day fixed upon to commence the bloody work, was the twenty-third of February, A.D. 303, that being the day in which the Terminalia were celebrated, and on which, as the cruel pagans boasted, they hoped to put a termination to Christianity. On the appointed day, the persecution began in Nicomedia, on the morning of which the prefect of that city repaired, with a great number of officers and assistants, to the church of the Christians, where, having forced open the doors, they seized upon all the sacred books, and committed them to the flames.

The whole of this transaction was in the presence of Diocletian and Galerius, who, not contented with burning the books, had the church levelled with the ground. This was followed by a severe edict, commanding the destruction of all other Christian churches and books; and an order soon succeeded, to render Christians of all denomination outlaws.

The publication of this edict occasioned an immediate martyrdom, for a bold Christian not only tore it down from the place to which it was affixed, but execrated the name of the emperor for his injustice. A provocation like this was sufficient to call down pagan vengeance upon his head; he was accordingly seized, severely tortured, and then burned alive.

All the Christians were apprehended and imprisoned; and Galerius privately ordered the imperial palace to be set on fire, that the Christians might be charged as the incendiaries, and a plausible pretence given for carrying on the persecution with the greater severities. A general sacrifice was commenced, which occasioned various martyrdoms. No distinction was made of age or sex; the name of Christian was so obnoxious to the pagans that all indiscriminately fell sacrifices to their opinions. Many houses were set on fire, and whole Christian families perished in the flames; and others had stones fastened about their necks, and being tied together were driven into the sea. The persecution became general in all the Roman provinces, but more particularly in the east; and as it lasted ten years, it is impossible to ascertain the numbers martyred, or to enumerate the various modes of martyrdom.

Racks, scourges, swords, daggers, crosses, poison, and famine, were made use of in various parts to dispatch the Christians; and invention was exhausted to devise tortures against such as had no crime, but thinking differently from the votaries of superstition.

A city of Phrygia, consisting entirely of Christians, was burnt, and all the inhabitants perished in the flames.

Tired with slaughter, at length, several governors of provinces represented to the imperial court, the impropriety of such conduct. Hence many were respited from execution, but, though they were not put to death, as much as possible was done to render their lives miserable, many of them having their ears cut off, their noses slit, their right eyes put out, their limbs rendered useless by dreadful dislocations, and their flesh seared in conspicuous places with red-hot irons.

It is necessary now to particularize the most conspicious persons who laid down their lives in martyrdom in this bloody persecution.

Sebastian, a celebrated martyr, was born at Narbonne, in Gaul, instructed in the principles of Christianity at Milan, and afterward became an officer of the emperor's guard at Rome. He remained a true Christian in the midst of idolatry; unallured by the splendors of a court, untained by evil examples, and uncontaminated by the hopes of preferment. Refusing to be a pagan, the emperor ordered him to be taken to a field near the city, termed the Campus Martius, and there to be shot to death with arrows; which sentence was executed accordingly. Some pious Christians coming to the place of execution, in order to give his body burial, perceived signs of life in him, and immediately moving him to a place of security, they, in a short time effected his recovery, and prepared him for a second martyrdom; for, as soon as he was able to go out, he placed himself intentionally in the emperor's way as he was going to the temple, and reprehended him for his various cruelties and unreasonable prejudices against Christianity. As soon as Diocletian had overcome his surprise, he ordered Sebastian to be seized, and carried to a place near the palace, and beaten to death; and, that the Christians should not either use means again to recover or bury his body, he ordered that it should be thrown into the common sewer. Nevertheless, a Christian lady named Lucina, found means to remove it from the sewer, and bury it in the catacombs, or repositories of the dead.

The Christians, about this time, upon mature consideration, thought it unlawful to bear arms under a heathen emperor. Maximilian, the son of Fabius Victor, was the first beheaded under this regulation.

Vitus, a Sicilian of considerable family, was brought up a Christian; when his virtues increased with his years, his constancy supported him under all afflictions, and his faith was superior to the most dangerous perils. His father, Hylas, who was a pagan, finding that he had been instructed in the principles of Christianity by the nurse who brought him up, used all his endeavors to bring him back to paganism, and at length sacrificed his son to the idols, June 14, A.D. 303.

Victor was a Christian of a good family at Marseilles, in France; he spent a great part of the night in visiting the afflicted, and confirming the weak; which pious work he could not, consistently with his own safety, perform in the daytime; and his fortune he spent in relieving the distresses of poor Christians. He was at length, however, seized by the emperor Maximian's decree, who ordered him to be bound, and dragged through the streets. During the execution of this order, he was treated with all manner of cruelties and indignities by the enraged populace. Remaining still inflexible, his courage was deemed obstinacy. Being by order stretched upon the rack, he turned his eyes toward heaven, and prayed to God to endue him with patience, after which he underwent the tortures with most admirable fortitude. After the executioners were tired with inflicting torments on him, he was conveyed to a dungeon. In his confinement, he converted his jailers, named Alexander, Felician, and Longinus. This affair coming to the ears of the emperor, he ordered them immediately to be put to death, and the jailers were accordingly beheaded. Victor was then again put to the rack, unmercifully beaten with batoons, and again sent to prison. Being a third time examined concerning his religion, he persevered in his principles; a small altar was then brought, and he was commanded to offer incense upon it immediately. Fired with indignation at the request, he boldly stepped forward, and with his foot overthrew both altar and idol. This so enraged the emperor Maximian, who was present, that he ordered the foot with which he had kicked the altar to be immediately cut off; and Victor was thrown into a mill, and crushed to pieces with the stones, A.D. 303.

Maximus, governor of Cilicia, being at Tarsus, three Christians were brought before him; their names were Tarachus, an aged man, Probus, and Andronicus. After repeated tortures and exhortations to recant, they, at length, were ordered for execution.

Being brought to the amphitheater, several beasts were let loose upon them; but none of the animals, though hungry, would touch them. The keeper then brought out a large bear, that had that very day destroyed three men; but this voracious creature and a fierce lioness both refused to touch the prisoners. Finding the design of destroying them by the means of wild beasts ineffectual, Maximus ordered them to be slain by the sword, on October 11, A.D. 303.

Romanus, a native of Palestine, was deacon of the church of Caesarea at the time of the commencement of Diocletian's persecution. Being condemned for his faith at Antioch, he was scourged, put to the rack, his body torn with hooks, his flesh cut with knives, his face scarified, his teeth beaten from their sockets, and his hair plucked up by the roots. Soon after he was ordered to be strangled, November 17, A.D. 303.

Susanna, the niece of Caius, bishop of Rome, was pressed by the emperor Diocletian to marry a noble pagan, who was nearly related to him. Refusing the honor intended her, she was beheaded by the emperor's order.

Dorotheus, the high chamberlain of the household to Diocletian, was a Christian, and took great pains to make converts. In his religious labors, he was joined by

Gorgonius, another Christian, and one belonging to the palace. They were first tortured and then strangled.

Peter, a eunuch belonging to the emperor, was a Christian of singular modesty and humility. He was laid on a gridiron, and broiled over a slow fire until he expired.

Cyprian, known by the title of the magician, to distinguish him from Cyprian, bishop of Carthage, was a native of Natioch. He received a liberal education in his youth, and particularly applied himself to astrology; after which he traveled for improvement through Greece, Egypt, India, etc. In the course of time he became acquainted with Justina, a young lady of Antioch, whose birth, beauty, and accomplishments, rendered her the admiration of all who knew her. A pagan gentleman applied to Cyprian, to promote his suit with the beautiful Justina; this he undertook, but soon himself became converted, burnt his books of astrology and magic, received baptism, and felt animated with a powerful spirit of grace. The conversion of Cyprian had a great effect on the pagan gentleman who paid his addresses to Justina, and he in a short time embraced Christianity. During the persecutions of Diocletian, Cyprian and Justina were seized upon as Chrisitans, the former was torn with pincers, and the latter chastised; and, after suffering other torments, both were beheaded.

Eulalia, a Spanish lady of a Christian family, was remarkable in her youth for sweetness of temper, and solidity of understanding seldom found in the capriciousness of juvenile years. Being apprehended as a Christian, the magistrate attempted by the mildest means, to bring her over to paganism, but she ridiculed the pagan deities with such asperity, that the judge, incensed at her behavior, ordered her to be tortured. Her sides were accordingly torn by hooks, and her breasts burnt in the most shocking manner, until she expired by the violence of the flames, December, A.D. 303.

In the year 304, when the persecution reached Spain, Dacian, the governor of Terragona, ordered Valerius the bishop, and Vincent the deacon, to be seized, loaded with irons, and imprisoned. The prisoners being firm in their resolution, Valerius was banished, and Vincent was racked, his limbs dislocated, his flesh torn with hooks, and he was laid on a gridiron, which had not only a fire placed under it, but spikes at the top, which ran into his flesh. These torments neither destroying him, nor changing his resolutions, he was remanded to prison, and confined in a small, loathsome, dark dungeon, strewed with sharp flints, and pieces of broken glass, where he died, January 22, 304. His body was thrown into the river.

The persecution of Diocletian began particularly to rage in A.D. 304, when many Christians were put to cruel tortures and the most painful and ignominious deaths; the most eminent and paritcular of whom we shall enumerate.

Saturninus, a priest of Albitina, a town of Africa, after being tortured, was remanded to prison, and there starved to death. His four children, after being variously tormented, shared the same fate with their father.

Dativas, a noble Roman senator; Thelico, a pious Christian; Victoria, a young lady of considerable family and fortune, with some others of less consideration, all auditors of Saturninus, were tortured in a similar manner, and perished by the same means.

Agrape, Chionia, and Irene, three sisters, were seized upon at Thessalonica, when Diocletian's persecution reached Greece. They were burnt, and received the crown of martyrdom in the flames, March 25, A.D. 304. The governor, finding that he could make no impression on Irene, ordered her to be exposed naked in the streets, which shameful order having been executed, a fire was kindled near the city wall, amidst whose flames her spirit ascended beyond the reach of man's cruelty.

Agatho, a man of a pious turn of mind, with Cassice, Philippa, and Eutychia, were martyred about the same time; but the particulars have not been transmitted to us.

Marcellinus, bishop of Rome, who succeeded Caius in that see, having strongly opposed paying divine honors to Diocletian, suffered martyrdom, by a variety of tortures, in the year 324, conforting his soul until he expired with the prospect of these glorious rewards it would receive by the tortures suffered in the body.

Victorius, Carpophorus, Severus, and Severianus, were brothers, and all four employed in places of great trust and honor in the city of Rome. Having exclaimed against the worship of idols, they were apprehended, and scourged, with the plumbetae, or scourges, to the ends of which were fastened leaden balls. This punishment was exercised with such excess of cruelty that the pious brothers fell martyrs to its severity.

Timothy, a deacon of Mauritania, and Maura his wife, had not been united together by the bands of wedlock above three weeks, when they were separated from each other by the persecution. Timothy, being apprehended, as a Christian, was carried before Arrianus, the governor of Thebais, who, knowing that he had the keeping of the Holy Scriptures, commanded him to deliver them up to be burnt; to which he answered, "Had I children, I would sooner deliver them up to be sacrificed, than part with the Word of God." The governor being much incensed at this reply, ordered his eyes to be put out, with red-hot irons, saying, "The books shall at least be useless to you, for you shall not see to read them." His patience under the operation was so great that the governor grew more exasperated; he, therefore, in order, if possible, to overcome his fortitude, ordered him to be hung up by the feet, with a weight tied about his neck, and a gag in his mouth. In this state, Maura his wife, tenderly urged him for her sake to recant; but, when the gag was taken out of his mouth, instead of consenting to his wife's entreaties, he greatly blamed her mistaken love, and declared his resolution of dying for the faith. The consequence was, that Maura resolved to imitate his courage and fidelity and either to accompany or follow him to glory. The governor, after trying in vain to alter her resolution, ordered her to be tortured, which was executed with great severity. After this, Timothy and Maura were crucified near each other, A.D. 304.

Sabinus, bishop of Assisium, refusing to sacrifice to Jupiter, and pushing the idol from him, had his hand cut off by the order of the governor of Tuscany. While in prison, he converted the governor and his family, all of whom suffered martyrdom for the faith. Soon after their execution, Sabinus himself was scourged to death, December, A.D. 304.

Tired with the farce of state and public business, the emperor Diocletian resigned the imperial diadem, and was succeeded by Constantius and Galerius; the former a prince of the most mild and humane disposition and the latter equally remarkable for his cruelty and tyranny. These divided the empire into two equal governments, Galerius ruling in the east, and Constantius in the west; and the people in the two governments felt the effects of the dispositions of the two emperors; for those in the west were governed in the mildest manner, but such as resided in the east felt all the miseries of oppression and lengthened tortures.

Among the many martyred by the order of Galerius, we shall enumerate the most eminent.

Amphianus was a gentleman of eminence in Lucia, and a scholar of Eusebius; Julitta, a Lycaonian of royal descent, but more celebrated for her virtues than noble blood. While on the rack, her child was killed before her face. Julitta, of Cappadocia, was a lady of distinguished capacity, great virtue, and uncommon courage. To complete the execution, Julitta had boiling pitch poured on her feet, her sides torn with hooks, and received the conclusion of her martyrdom, by being beheaded, April 16, A.D. 305.

Hermolaus, a venerable and pious Christian, or a great age, and an intimate acquaintance of Panteleon's, suffered martyrdom for the faith on the same day, and in the same manner as Panteleon.

Eustratius, secretary to the governor of Armina, was thrown into a fiery furnace for exhorting some Christians who had been apprehended, to persevere in their faith.

Nicander and Marcian, two eminent Roman military officers, were apprehended on account of their faith. As they were both men of great abilities in their profession, the utmost means were used to induce them to renounce Christianity; but these endeavors being found ineffectual, they were beheaded.

In the kingdom of Naples, several martyrdoms took place, in particular, Januaries, bishop of Beneventum; Sosius, deacon of Misene; Proculus, another deacon; Eutyches and Acutius, two laymen; Festus, a deacon; and Desiderius, a reader; all, on account of being Christians, were condemned by the governor of Campania to be devoured by the wild beasts. The savage animals, however, would not touch them, and so they were beheaded.

Quirinus, bishop of Siscia, being carried before Matenius, the governor, was ordered to sacrifice to the pagan deities, agreeably to the edicts of various Roman emperors. The governor, perceiving his constancy, sent him to jail, and ordered him to be heavily ironed; flattering himself, that the hardships of a jail, some occasional tortures and the weight of chains, might overcome his resolution. Being decided in his principles, he was sent to Amantius, the principal governor of Pannonia, now Hungary, who loaded him with chains, and carried him through the principal towns of the Danube, exposing him to ridicule wherever he went. Arriving at length at Sabaria, and finding that Quirinus would not renounce his faith, he ordered him to be cast into a river, with a stone fastened about his neck. This sentence being put into execution, Quirinus floated about for some time, and, exhorting the people in the most pious terms, concluded his admonitions with this prayer: "It is no new thing, O all-powerful Jesus, for Thee to stop the course of rivers, or to cause a man to walk upon the water, as Thou didst Thy servant Peter; the people have already seen the proof of Thy power in me; grant me now to lay down my life for Thy sake, O my God." On pronouncing the last words he immediately sank, and died, June 4, A.D. 308. His body was afterwards taken up, and buried by some pious Christians.

Pamphilus, a native of Phoenicia, of a considerable family, was a man of such extensive learning that he was called a second Origen. He was received into the body of the clergy at Caesarea, where he established a public library and spent his time in the practice of every Christian virtue. He copied the greatest part of the works of Origen with his own hand, and, assisted by Eusebius, gave a correct copy of the Old Testament, which had suffered greatly by the ignorance or negligence of former transcribers. In the year 307, he was apprehended, and suffered torture and martyrdom.

Marcellus, bishop of Rome, being banished on account of his faith, fell a martyr to the miseries he suffered in exile, January 16, A.D. 310.

Peter, the sixteenth bishop of Alexandria, was martyred November 25, A.D. 311, by order of Maximus Caesar, who reigned in the east.

Agnes, a virgin of only thirteen years of age, was beheaded for being a Christian; as was Serene, the empress of Diocletian. Valentine, a priest, suffered the same fate at Rome; and Erasmus, a bishop, was martyred in Campania.

Soon after this the persecution abated in the middle parts of the empire, as well as in the west; and Providence at length began to manifest vengeance on the persecutors. Maximian endeavored to corrupt his daughter Fausta to murder Constantine her husband; which she discovered, and Constantine forced him to choose his own death, when he preferred the ignominious death of hanging after being an emperor near twenty years.

Constantine was the good and virtuous child of a good and virtuous father, born in Britain. His mother was named Helena, daughter of King Coilus. He was a most bountiful and gracious prince, having a desire to nourish learning and good arts, and did oftentimes use to read, write, and study himself. He had marvellous good success and prosperous achieving of all things he took in hand, which then was (and truly) supposed to proceed of this, for that he was so great a favorer of the Christian faith. Which faith when he had once embraced, he did ever after most devoutly and religiously reverence.

Thus Constantine, sufficiently appointed with strength of men but especially with strength of God, entered his journey coming towards Italy, which was about the last year of the persecution, A.D. 313. Maxentius, understanding of the coming of Constantine, and trusting more to his devilish art of magic than to the good will of his subjects, which he little deserved, durst not show himself out of the city, nor encounter him in the open field, but with privy garrisons laid wait for him by the way in sundry straits, as he should come; with whom Constantine had divers skirmishes, and by the power of the Lord did ever vanquish them and put them to flight.

Notwithstanding, Constantine yet was in no great comfort, but in great care and dread in his mind (approaching now near unto Rome) for the magical charms and sorceries of Maxentius, wherewith he had vanquished before Severus, sent by Galerius against him. Wherefore, being in great doubt and perplexity in himself, and revolving many things in his mind, what help he might have against the operations of his charming, Constantine, in his journey drawing toward the city, and casting up his eyes many times to heaven, in the south part, about the going down of the sun, saw a great brightness in heaven, appearing in the similitude of a cross, giving this inscription, In hoc vince, that is, "In this overcome."

Eusebius Pamphilus doth witness that he had heard the said Constantine himself oftentimes report, and also to swear this to be true and certain, which he did see with his own eyes in heaven, and also his soldiers about him. At the sight whereof when he was greatly astonished, and consulting with his men upon the meaning thereof, behold, in the night season in his sleep, Christ appeared to him with the sign of the same cross which he had seen before, bidding him to make the figuration thereof, and to carry it in his wars before him, and so should we have the victory.

Constantine so established the peace of the Church that for the space of a thousand years we read of no set persecution against the Christians, unto the time of John Wickliffe.

So happy, so glorious was this victory of Constantine, surnamed the Great! For the joy and gladness whereof, the citizens who had sent for him before, with exceeding triumph brought him into the city of Rome, where he was most honorably received, and celebrated the space of seven days together; having, moreover, in the market place, his image set up, holding in his right hand the sign of the cross, with this inscription: "With this wholesome sign, the true token of fortitude, I have rescued and delivered our city from the yoke of the tyrant."

We shall conclude our account of the tenth and last general persecution with the death of St. George, the titular saint and patron of England. St. George was born in Cappadocia, of Christian parents; and giving proofs of his courage, was promoted in the army of the emperor Diocletian. During the persecution, St. George threw up his command, went boldly to the senate house, and avowed his being a Christian, taking occasion at the same time to remonstrate against paganism, and point out the absurdity of worshipping idols. This freedom so greatly provoked the senate that St. George was ordered to be tortured, and by the emperor's orders was dragged through the streets, and beheaded the next day.

The legend of the dragon, which is associated with this martyr, is usually illustrated by representing St. George seated upon a charging horse and transfixing the monster with his spear. This fiery dragon symbolizes the devil, who was vanquished by St. George's steadfast faith in Christ, which remained unshaken in spite of torture and death.[7]

What makes all this very interesting is what the first article above took note of. The Devil found out that he couldn't put an end to the Church through persecution. What we will find out in the next or third Church age through the letter sent to the angel of the church of Pergamum is that the Devil has switched tactics in the same exact way that he did through Balaam. He could not defeat them with a full frontal assault and violence. This only made the Church grow bigger.

As the saying goes, "If you can't beat them, join them." Meaning, as the tactics of Balaam dictate go into their camp, seduce them with sexual immorality and idolatry causing them to sin against their God and, therefore, be rejected by Him. The third Church age is a time when the Roman emperor, Constantine, became a Christian and Christianity eventually became the state religion of the Roman Empire. This marriage of the empire and the Church caused the ways of Balaam and the Nicolaitans to enter into the Church. With these tactical changes, the Devil has started destroying the Church during the third Church age from within. As we will see in the letter written to the angel of the church of Pergamum.

WEB 2 Co 5:14 *For the love of Christ constrains us; because we judge thus, that one died for all, therefore all died.* [15] *He died for all, that those who live should no longer live to themselves, but to him who for their sakes died and rose again . . .*

Note: The summary given by "Foxe's Book of Martyrs" of the persecution perpetrated in the Roman Empire was characterized in advance by Jesus saying:

NIV Rev 2:10 Do not be afraid of what you are about to suffer. I tell you, the devil will put some of you in prison to test you, and you will suffer persecution for ten days. Be faithful, even to the point of death, and I will give you the crown of life.

The important thing to take away from this is that although Jesus' words are direct, even somewhat cryptic, they are few. His words in these letters should not be overlooked as insignificant in scope. His words instead should be given the significance of the scope of history itself. They are sobering truths that define all of everything His Church will experience and endure from its beginning to its end.

Notes

[6] *The Church at Smyrna.* (n.d.). Retrieved October 2012, from Spiritjournals.com:
http://www.spiritjournals.com/Special%20Sections/Persecuted%20Church/Articles/smyrna.htm

[7] *Foxes' Book of Martyers: Chapter 2 The Ten Primitive Persecutions*(n.d.). Retrieved November 2017, from Christian Classics Ethereal Library:
http://www.ccel.org/f/foxe/martyrs/fox102.htm

.

CHAPTER 6

Pergamum

The Third Church Age

To the Church in Pergamum

WEB Rev 2:12 *"To the angel of the assembly* (church) *in Pergamum write:*
"He who has the sharp two-edged (double-edged) *sword says these things:*
¹³ "I know your works and where you dwell, where Satan's throne is. You hold firmly to my name, and didn't deny my faith in the days of Antipas my witness, my faithful one, who was killed among you, where Satan dwells. ¹⁴ But I have a few things against you, because you have there some who hold the teaching of Balaam, who taught Balak to throw a stumbling block before the children of Israel, to eat things sacrificed to idols, and to commit sexual immorality. ¹⁵ So you also have some who hold to the teaching of the Nicolaitans likewise. ¹⁶ Repent therefore, or else I am coming to you quickly, and I will make war against them with the sword of my mouth. ¹⁷ He who has an ear, let him hear what the Spirit says to the assemblies (churches). *To him who overcomes, to him I will give of the hidden manna, and I will give him a white stone, and on the stone a new name written, which no one knows but he who receives it.*

In verse 13 (above) it reads, "where Satan's throne is." In this city Pergamum was a temple where they worshipped Zeus. Zeus is the father or chief of the gods (fallen angels) and therefore Zeus is Satan, as Jesus refers to him. This town and its citizens worshiped Satan under the name of Zeus. Jesus was acknowledging that He realizes the Christians of this city had to contend and compete with Satan worship. The spiritual atmosphere of this city was charged with the seduction, lies, bondage, and a violent hostility towards the true God and His people. These circumstances are the regional and contemporary manifestation that this letter is directed towards concerning the church in Pergamum.

However, this letter is written to the third Church age as well as the third church. The second Church age was an age of persecution. The third Church age is an age of tolerance and acceptance. The seat of Satan may be in the city of Pergamum during the time of their tempting, however, on the grander scale of things the seat of the Roman Empire, Rome itself is the great city ruled by the Devil.

Note: It is important to keep in mind that so far we are talking about things which have already transpired in the past. However, at the same time, they are things which had not occurred at the time Jesus walked among the lampstands dictating these letters to John. Jesus predicted by saying in the letter to them, "what you are about to suffer. . . " John wrote Revelation during the reign of the emperor Domitian somewhere between the dates of AD 81–96. The outbreak of persecution Jesus predicted on the "second church", Smyrna, did not happen until 303 AD under the emperor Diocletian (the tenth and final emperor of Rome who persecuted the Church) ending 10 years later in 313 AD. However, the "second Church age" of persecution started long before, in 64 AD under the emperor Nero (the first of the ten emperors of Rome who persecuted the Church). That Church age will not have its global fulfillment until the 10 kings of the world imprison and kill the Christians under the beast during the great tribulation. However, the third Church age began in 313 AD when emperor Constantine brought tolerance and acceptance for the Christian religion.

The Christians of Pergamum had to endure in a city which had a temple and the people worshiped Zeus/Satan. However, in Rome itself, the headquarters and center of the Roman Empire, there is located on Capitoline one of the seven hills of Rome, the first temple to Jupiter built by the Romans. Zeus, the Greek name for this god, is known to the Romans as Jupiter, the chief of the gods. This temple was originally built in Rome in 509 BC. It was rebuilt three more times on the same site. The latest, or fourth time, was the largest and most lavish. It was rebuilt by the emperor Domitian. To give an idea of the opulence, it is recorded that Domitian gilded the bronze roof using about 850,000 pounds of gold.

Regarding the timeline, Domitian was the emperor when John wrote the book of Revelation. It was Domitian who persecuted John. The story goes that when John could not be killed by having been lowered into boiling oil, he was then exiled to the island of Patmos where John received the vision and wrote the book Revelation.

While John was writing this letter to Pergamum, emperor Domitian was rebuilding the temple of Jupiter/Zeus (more specifically, Satan) in Rome on the Capitoline hill. At the base of the Capitoline hill in Rome was the temple of Saturn the sun god, which is believed by many to be Nimrod, the beast and antichrist, who will come back from the dead. Right there on the seven hills was a temple for the Devil and his antichrist. Both of which have the same ordained destiny of seven heads, seven crowns, and ten horns. The Roman Empire was the sixth head and kingdom of the beast. In addition, Rome is the great city (the headquarters for) Babylon for both the sixth and seventh kingdoms of the beast.

Note: After Jerusalem and the temple of God were destroyed in 70 AD by the Romans, Jerusalem was renamed by the Romans as Capitoline. The name of the very same hill in Rome where those two temples (among others) were built. Furthermore, an attempt was made to build a temple for Zeus/Satan on the site where the temple of God was torn down. Although it was not time for this to happen, it was a prophetic foreshadowing of what is to come. Just like in the days of Antiochus when he sacrificed a pig to Zeus in the Temple desecrating it. Eventually, at the end, Jerusalem will serve as the great city, the headquarters of Babylon and of the beast/antichrist during the great tribulation.

The Jewish temple of God will be rebuilt once more before the beginning of the last 7 years of the 70-7's. Afterwards, that temple of God to come, will be used to worship and bring back from among the dead the agent of the Devil, the beast/Nimrod, the eighth king. After that is accomplished, Jerusalem will become the great city, the center for Babylon from where the beast rules the globe, as well as the ten kings and their ten districts comprising the entire globe.

As was pointed out, this Church age begins at the end of the Great Persecution, and the beginning of Christian tolerance through the reign of Constantine, emperor of the Roman Empire. He became a Christian and got deeply involved in Christian affairs resulting in the Church becoming the state religion. Circumstances swung from one extreme to the other. This married the Roman Empire to the Church. Jesus says to this church angel:

WEB Rev 2:13 *"I know your works and where you dwell, where Satan's throne is. You hold firmly to my name, and didn't deny my faith in the days of Antipas my witness, my faithful one, who was killed among you, where Satan dwells."*

In looking at what Jesus says as the third Church age, two things are important to note here. One, He recognizes that the Christians dwell where Satan's throne is. This is a reference to the fact that they live in Babylon/the Roman Empire. The throne of the Roman Emperor is the throne of the beast and the throne of Satan. Jesus is acknowledging that they live in and among the government of the beast. Why is this important to mention at this point, given that the entire history of the Christian Church to date has been under the Roman Empire? We will see the answer to this question in the very next words Jesus speaks.

WEB Rev 2:13 *"I know your works and where you dwell, where Satan's throne is. You hold firmly to my name, and didn't deny my faith in the days of Antipas my witness, my faithful one, who was killed among you, where Satan dwells."*

In the martial arts of Judo, one's weight is used against them. If an opponent uses his strength and weight trying to overcome you, instead of fighting by pushing back, you pull him in the same direction his momentum is traveling in, while redirecting it slightly in the direction you want him to go. Then it is by his own power and momentum redirected by you which slams him into the ground.

What Jesus is referring to in the second half of this quote is: The tenness of persecution the Christians had to endure during the previous Church age leading up to this age of tolerance. The next statement He makes is to point out how "some" now have let the teachings of Balaam and the way of the Nicolaitans into the Church.

In this third Church age, the Roman Empire, more specifically Constantine, the emperor, has not only become a Christian, but has begun to involve himself in Church affairs in a significant manner starting with the Council of Nicaea in 325AD. He wanted to use Christianity to bind the hearts and minds of his empire together by making it the state religion. When he learned of conflicting doctrines which were having a dividing effect on the church, he could not have it.

Constantine, at his own personal expense, invited every Christian bishop in the world along with their entourages to Nicaea in order to come into agreement concerning this issue. Although Constantine let the bishops decide what was right, he hosted and presided over the event. He also enforced their decisions by exiling the offending bishop as well as threatened to do the same to those last hold outs who were slow to come into agreement with the majority of the bishops. This was the very first council of many which began to regulate and enforce a centralized and single Christian doctrine. The Church government was now consolidating and forming under the direction and model of the government of the beast—the Roman Empire—as designed by Constantine.

The point Jesus is trying to get across while speaking in future tense before it actually happens is this: He is acknowledging how well the Church stood fast during the age of persecution, the second Church age. Then after making an acknowledgment of that He points out that the Roman Empire is the throne of the Devil and his beast. Jesus said "some" have opened the door for Balaam and the Nicolaitans.

That "some," are the 300 bishops who attended that council and thereby inviting Rome into the Church to participate in and help form the Church government. Thus entered in the Church the spirit of Babylon. Jesus said "some" because 1,500 bishops who represented the majority of the Church in the world did not see fit to attend that council hosted by the Roman emperor.

Although it was over the course of several emperors who sat on the throne of Satan that the collaboration between the empire of Rome and the Church developed, this Council of Nicaea is when the spirit of Babylon and Balaam entered into the Church as arranged and seduced by Constantine. This age of tolerance and prosperity and the Church's rise to power over the nations marks the beginning of the third Church age 325 AD.

Why bring up "**the teachings**" of Balaam and "**the ways**" of the Nicolaitans?

The doctrine of Balaam:

WEB Rev 2:14 "You have there some who hold to the teaching of Balaam . . ."

> Notice that their teachings are comparable or the same as the doctrine of Balaam, the arch apostate deceiver and prophet who tried to divine magic against Israel when they came out of Egypt. When God would not allow him to place a curse on Israel, he later taught the Midianites and their allies to "seduce" Israel from their faithfulness to God, by sending their daughters and wives to use their sexual charms on them, and to entice them to commit immorality and the partake of pagan festivities and idolatrous worship, combining paganism with the worship of God – something which God abominates and thoroughly detests! The blending of the truth of God with paganism and wicked pagan festivals and practices is an abhorrence to God. It is called religious "syncretism."[8]

The teachings of Balaam are instructions on how to get the people of God, who are blessed and can't be cursed, to bring curses on themselves through seducing them into committing abominations and adulteries against the Lord. The reason Jesus brought up "the teachings of Balaam" and "the ways of the Nicolaitans" is because He was trying to warn this Church age that as this age of tolerance comes, don't be seduced by it. Remember, the Roman Empire is the seat and kingdom of the Devil and his beast—it is Babylon. Just because they are being nice to you and want to help you, doesn't mean they are right. They are by every account the empirical government of the Devil and his beast, no matter how tolerant and helpful they may be.

This tactic of the Devil, we will see, is what led to the downfall of the Church and its corruption. From the previous letter the Devil made things worse for his own objectives by persecuting Christians because the result was they only multiplied all the more. The more he killed, the more rose up. The enmity that God needs between the two lines of offspring was widening, becoming more defined as a result. People were brought to a valley of decision and clear choices had to be made on where one stands.

In this letter, Jesus starts off by saying to this church they were faithful in persecution. So the next test of the Devil is to try to bring corruption into their ranks so they pollute themselves and lose their place in heaven. A strategy that narrows that wide gap and blurs that which the enmity helps keep separated. Thus, the teachings of Balaam. The pagan practices of the Roman Empire was mixed with Christianity during this Church age. In his policies of Christian tolerance and restoration, as well as involvement, Constantine is the one who perpetrates the teachings of Balaam which seduce the Church. The sexually immoral ways of the Nicolaitans who blended their Christianity with the sexual cult practices of the Romans, are a result of his acceptance into the affairs of church leadership.

Note: Constantine waited until the day he died before receiving baptism. The strategy was that he did not want to sin after baptism and chance losing his salvation. He had still practiced some of the ways of the Roman cults and the worshiping of the sun god (Nimrod) until that day. He too mixed his beliefs and contributed greatly towards the Church doing so by the instituting of his laws which helped mix feast days of the pagans to that of the Church, the changing of the Sabbath day from Saturday to Sunday.

This Church age, the third Church age, is the planting of the darnel by the enemy (the Devil) which Jesus spoke of in His parable:

Amp Mt 13:24 ... *The kingdom of heaven is like a man who sowed good seed in his field.*
Amp Mt 13:25 *But while he was sleeping, his enemy came and sowed also darnel (weeds resembling wheat) among the wheat, and went on his way.*
Amp Mt 13:26 *So when the plants sprouted and formed grain, the darnel (weeds) appeared also*
Amp Mt 13:27 *And the servants of the owner came to him and said, Sir, did you not sow good seed in your field? Then how does it have darnel shoots in it?*
Amp Mt 13:28 *He replied to them, An enemy has done this. The servants said to him, Then do you want us to go and weed them out?*
Amp Mt 13:29 *But he said, No, lest in gathering the wild wheat (weeds resembling wheat), you root up the [true] wheat along with it.*
Amp Mt 13:30 *Let them grow together until the harvest; and at harvest time I will say to the reapers, Gather the darnel first and bind it in bundles to be burned, but gather the wheat into my granary.*

> Darnel usually grows in the same production zones as wheat and was a serious weed of cultivation until modern sorting machinery enabled darnel seeds to be separated efficiently from seed wheat. The similarity between these two plants is so great that

in some regions, darnel is referred to as "false wheat". It bears a close resemblance to wheat until the ear appears. The spikes of L. temulentum are more slender than those of wheat. The spikelets are oriented edgeways to the rachis and have only a single glume, while those of wheat are oriented with the flat side to the rachis and have two glumes. The wheat will also appear brown when ripe, whereas the darnel is black.

The French word for darnel is ivraie (from Latin ebriacus, intoxicated), which expresses the drunken nausea from eating the infected plant, which can be fatal. The French name echoes the scientific name, Latin temulentus "drunk."[9]

Note: Roman law prohibited sowing darnel among the wheat of an enemy, suggesting that the scenario presented here is realistic. Many translations use "weeds" instead of "tares".

What an incredible allegory Jesus has made! The enemy, Satan, has planted among the Christian community, darnel. The corruption of the pagan world and the empire of the beast has infiltrated the Church. It is a poison. Jesus hesitates to do something because it is difficult to tell apart the wheat from the darnel. That is when they are seeds, or immature plants, however, Jesus realizes once they mature, the wheat and the darnel are easily distinguishable from each other. The *Church Corrupt*, although they are Christian, when their corruption blossoms and matures over time will show itself as black. Conversely, the *Church Pure* when fully mature over time will show itself as beautiful golden brown—waves of amber swaying in the wind.

Jesus tells us it is at the harvest, both the *Church Pure* and the *Church Corrupt* will finally be separated so they might be distinguished from each other. The former Jesus will gather them to His barns, He will rapture and make them celestial humans. Of the latter, He says He "will make war against them with the sword of my mouth." The *Church Corrupt* will endure the great tribulation and their place in the world will be totally destroyed. However, as Paul says, they will be saved eventually but only as one who has passed through (the) fire (of the great tribulation). Then afterwards, they will become celestial humans who will comprise the great multitude (if when in that fire they are true to their testimony in Christ).

AmpICo 3:13 The work of each [one] will become [plainly, openly] known (shown for what it is); for the day [of Christ] will disclose and declare it, because it will be revealed with fire, and the fire will test and critically appraise the character and worth of the work each person has done.

AmpICo 3:14 If the work which any person has built on this Foundation [any product of his efforts whatever] survives [this test], he will get his reward.

AmpICo 3:15 But if any person's work is burned up [under the test], he will suffer the loss [of it all, losing his reward], though he himself will be saved, but only as [one who has passed] through fire.

Amp 1Co 3:16 Do you not discern and understand that you [the whole church at Corinth] are God's temple (His sanctuary), and that God's Spirit has His permanent dwelling in you [to be at home in you, collectively as a church and also individually]?

amp 1Co 3:17 If anyone does hurt to God's temple or corrupts it [with false doctrines] or destroys it, God will do hurt to him and bring him to the corruption of death and destroy him. For the temple of God is holy (sacred to Him) and that [temple] you [the believing church and its individual believers] are.

The Third Church Age

For: *"I know your works and where you dwell, where Satan's throne is. You hold firmly to my name, and didn't deny my faith in the days of Antipas my witness, my faithful one, who was killed among you, where Satan dwells."*

> The Great Alter of Pergamon is in the Pergamon Museum, Berlin. The base of this altar remains on the upper part of the Acropolis. It was perhaps this altar, believed to be dedicated to Zeus, that John of Patmos referred to as "Satan's Throne" in his Book of Revelation.[10]

> According to Christian tradition, John the Apostle ordained Antipas as bishop of Pergamon during the reign of the Roman emperor Domitian. The traditional account goes on to say Antipas was martyred in 92 AD by burning in a brazen bull-shaped altar.[11]

Again, Jesus is giving this church credit for being strong and faithful in the face of persecution during the second Church age, the age of persecution. However, next we see how the Devil's plan to infiltrate the ranks with seducing sinful people unwilling to fully conform to God's will. They call themselves Christ followers, however, they co-mingle the ways of the Roman Empire and the Christian Church in this third Church age.

Against/warning: *"But I have a few things against you, because you have there some who hold the teaching of Balaam, who taught Balak to throw a stumbling block before the children of Israel, to eat things sacrificed to idols, and to commit sexual immorality."* *WEB Rev 2:15 So you also have some who hold to the teaching of the Nicolaitans likewise.* *WEB Rev 2:16 Repent therefore!"*

"Repent therefore!" In the first Church age they hated the people who tried to seduce the Church into sin through the teachings of Balaam, and the doctrines of the Nicolaitans. However, in spite of the warnings of Jesus to the first Church age losing sight of their first love has opened this age to being seduced like the Israelites which caused 34,000 to die that day. The dying stopped at that number only because Phinehas, grandson of Aaron, made a radical gesture of repentance intervening with intercession.

Why would losing sight of your first love open one up to being deceived and seduced by these doctrines?

Think about it, when you are interested in doing your own will, gratifying your own desires and not that of Jesus', it is only natural that something that would appeal to your own desires would seem right. Like, for example, to be able to have sex as a part of Lovefeast. After all, some might think; "It is called a 'love' feast, and everybody else in the world is doing it."

Amp Jn 7:17 If any man desires to do His will (God's pleasure), he will know (have the needed illumination to recognize, and can tell for himself) whether the teaching is from God . . .

If in your very essence your essential motive is to do the will of God, pleasing Him and you are not conflicted, what seems right in your own heart will end up being God's will. However, if in your very essence your essential motive is to do your own will and please yourself, well then, what ends up seeming right in your heart will be not the things of God, but what ultimately satisfies your own desires. As a result, things that are just simply wrong, seem to make perfect sense because of a desire to do your own will and having lost your first love—to do the will of Jesus. Believe it or not, it is just that simple!

What we hold dear in our hearts always is revealed by what we believe and embrace as right. Therefore, no one is innocent, no one is simply deceived. Like the old saying goes, "You cannot fool an honest man." We might sit there and plead with God because we were tricked, but God knows why we were tricked. It is because in our heart of hearts, we want to serve ourselves, and not Him. That makes us guilty, and there is no way to mask it. This is exactly why losing our first love unwittingly opens us up to everything that is evil and everything that separates us from God.

It is easy to recognize that the Church was being highly persecuted in fear of their lives, but possessed Jesus as their first love and as such, willingly gave up their lives causing the Church to grow in numbers. It's even more understandable that when the very people who were killing them wanted to be friends with them, it would be easy to be deceived into accepting Babylon into the Church. It is important for us to see how it is true that losing your first love leads to every other deception, seducing us while seemingly making perfect sense to do so.

It was the fear of death and self-preservation that made it seem like a good thing to come in league with Babylon/the Roman Empire. If fear of death and self-preservation rules the heart, it has to be said, your first love has become your own life and it is no longer Jesus'. After this transition, it is easy to see how every arrangement made between Babylon and the Church would make sense; even seem like God's will. That is because it would usher in peace, preservation of life, and prosperity. That is keeping in mind what was taught earlier, if anyone desires to do God's will (with their whole heart), then what seems right to that person will be God's will. Likewise, if anyone desires to do their own will, in their heart what will seem right is what serves their own will and desires.

"Losing your first love" has led the Church, over time, to be deceived by the very things they were wise to and at one time hated. That was the first Church age's one redeeming factor; "at least you hate them as I do." However, this Church age no longer has even that! Things are going from bad to worse! That is because the "them" the first Church age hated was the Roman Empire and its government. They saw it as Babylon. There was enmity between them. But now this Church age is deceived into thinking the Roman Empire and its emperor Constantine (who is Babylon and the throne of the Devil) are their salvation because of their help and tolerance.

Jesus sees this coming, though He can only warn His beloved bride before He finds it necessary to take action. It is piling up, He will divorce us and come against and fight those in the Church who participate, those who lead astray, and those who stand by and do nothing while it happens! At least with the Jews, someone did something to put an end to the madness.

The Double-edged sword:

Words that give life: *"... To him who overcomes, to him I will give of the hidden manna, and I will give him a white stone, and on the stone a new name written, which no one knows but he who receives it."*

The words that give judgment: *"... or else I am coming to you quickly, and I will make war against them with the sword of my mouth."*

The characteristics of His person to this church: *" ... He who has the sharp two-edged sword says these things."*

The sad fact is that even though some through history repent from these ways and even return to their first love, this error, once introduced, continues to broaden in scope of influence and grow taller in time, to the end of the Church ages. Even if this error has non-sexual expressions of this spirit of whoredom and adultery, it is still among us to this day. The number of those who are pure compared to those who are corrupt are small and getting smaller. We will see soon in these letters that these errors take so much of the Church that the errors in the Church become the new normal. The infrastructure of the Church is so corrupt, it becomes beyond fixing and has to be done away with.

Notes

[8] Dankenbring, W. (n.d.). *Who are the "Nicolaitans"*. Retrieved October 2012, from TriumphPro.com:

www.triumphpro.com/nicolaitans.htm

[9] *Lolium temulentum*. (2017, September 20). Retrieved December 2017, from Wikipedia, The Free Encylopedia:

https://en.wikipedia.org/wiki/Lolium_temulentum

[10] *Pergamon*. (2013, August 16). Retrieved August 2013, from Wikipedia, The Free Encyclopedia:

http://en.wikipedia.org/wiki/Pergamon

[11] *Antipas of Pergamum*. (2013, March 6). Retrieved August 2013, from Wikipedia, The Free Encylopedia:

http://en.wikipedia.org/wiki/Antipas_of_Pergamum

CHAPTER 7

Thyatira

The Fourth Church Age

To the Church in Thyatira

WEB Rev 2:18 *"To the angel of the assembly* (church) *in Thyatira write:*
"The Son of God, who has his eyes like a flame of fire, and his feet are like burnished brass
(bronze), *says these things:*
¹⁹ "I know your works, your love, faith, service, patient endurance, and that your last works
are more than the first. ²⁰ But I have this against you, that you tolerate your (that) *woman,*
Jezebel, who calls herself a prophetess. She teaches and seduces my servants to commit sexual
immorality, and to eat things sacrificed to idols. ²¹ I gave her time to repent, but she refuses to
repent of her sexual immorality. ²² Behold, I will throw her into a bed (of suffering), *and*
those who commit adultery with her into great oppression, unless they repent of her works. ²³
I will kill her children with Death, and all the assemblies will know that I am he who searches
the minds and hearts. I will give to each one of you according to your deeds. ²⁴ But to you I
say, to the rest who are in Thyatira, as many as don't have this teaching, who don't know
what some call 'the deep things of Satan,' to you I say, I am not putting any other burden on
you. ²⁵ Nevertheless, hold that which you have firmly until I come. ²⁶ He who overcomes, and
he who keeps my works to the end, to him I will give authority over the nations. ²⁷ He will
rule them with a rod of iron, shattering them like clay pots; as I also have received of my
Father: ²⁸ and I will give him the morning star. ²⁹ He who has an ear, let him hear what the
Spirit says to the assemblies (churches).

The fourth Church age is the most profoundly pivotal of all the Church ages.

In the previous letter, the Lord brought up the teaching of Balaam who taught Balak
to throw a stumbling block before the children of Israel. He seduced them into
eating things sacrificed to idols and to commit sexual immorality. This was an Old
Testament occurrence. Likewise, the Lord bought up the ways of the Nicolaitans

who are a contemporary example of those who actually have homogenized those same immoral pagan practices of the Romans into their Christianity. God tells us in the first letter that He is against these Nicolaitans who have done so. In fact, the Lord praises the first Church for rejecting them and their detestable practices. The first Church did not give the Nicolaitans acceptance without conformity.

However, now in this fourth letter there are some who have let these things in and are ok with practicing them. They have given acceptance without conformity. After having admonished about the teachings of Balaam and the ways of the Nicolaitans in the previous letters, in this fourth letter and Church age the Lord speaks of Jezebel.

Jezebel is another Old Testament example which brought disaster upon the people of God for their tolerance of and submission to her. She was the queen of the northern kingdom, Israel. The king of Israel had married the princess of a foreign country who practiced detestable idolatrous ways. Thereby, king Ahab introduced these same ways to the Israelites by becoming married to her.

Jezebel:

Amp 1Ki 16:29 *In the thirty-eighth year of Asa king of Judah, Ahab son of Omri began his reign of twenty-two years over Israel in Samaria.*
Amp 1Ki 16:30 *And Ahab son of Omri did evil in the sight of the Lord above all before him.*
Amp 1Ki 16:31 *As if it had been a light thing for Ahab to walk in the sins of Jeroboam son of Nebat, he took for a wife Jezebel daughter of Ethbaal king of the Sidonians, and served Baal and worshiped him.*
Amp 1Ki 16:32 *He erected an altar for Baal in the house of Baal which he built in Samaria.*
Amp 1Ki 16:33 *And Ahab made an Asherah [idolatrous symbol of the goddess Asherah]. Ahab did more to provoke the Lord, the God of Israel, to anger than all the kings of Israel before him.*
Amp 1Ki 16:34 *In his days, Hiel the Bethelite built Jericho. He laid its foundations at the cost of the life of Abiram his firstborn, and set up its gates with the loss of his youngest son Segub, according to the word of the Lord which He spoke through Joshua son of Nun*

Against the laws of God, Ahab married a foreign woman, Jezebel. She was the daughter of the king of Sidon. Ahab built temples for the Baals for her and turned the Israelites to worship them. Jezebel had the prophets of God killed and rose up

850 pagan prophets for Baal and Asherah. It is accepted that Baal is the same god as Saturn to the Romans. They both are Nimrod. The practices of Christmas has its origin in the worship of Nimrod who was born on December 25th long before Christ was born. Asherah is the same as Aphrodite and Ishtar or Easter. The practices of Easter have their origins in worship of her as the goddess of love and fertility. Below are verses in which God speaks to Ezekiel about the practices which surround the worship of Nimrod, Ishtar, and their son Tammuz who was proclaimed the risen Nimrod.

Amp Eze 8:14 *Then He brought me to the entrance of the north gate of the Lord's house; and behold, there sat women weeping for Tammuz [a Babylonian god, who was supposed to die annually and subsequently be resurrected].*

Amp Eze 8:15 *Then said [the Spirit] to me, Have you seen this, O son of man? Yet again you shall see greater abominations that they are committing.*

Amp Eze 8:16 *And He brought me to the inner court of the Lord's house; and behold, at the door of the temple of the Lord, between the porch and the bronze altar, were about twenty-five men with their backs to the temple of the Lord and their faces toward the east, and they were bowing themselves toward the east and worshiping the sun.*

Amp Eze 8:17 *Then [the Spirit] said to me, Have you seen this, O son of man? Is it too slight a thing to the house of Judah to commit the abominations which they commit here they are doing here, that they must fill the land with violence and turn back afresh to provoke Me to anger? And behold, they put the branch to their nose [actually, before their mouths, in superstitious worship]!*

Amp Eze 8:18 *Therefore I will deal in wrath; My eye will not spare, nor will I have pity; and though they cry in My ears with a loud voice, yet will I not hear them.*

NIV Eze 8:17a *. . . Is it a trivial matter for the house of Judah to do the detestable things ?*

Referred to in the above verses are the practices of Easter. Prayer, morning, fasting and self-mutilation for 40 days, so that Nimrod would rise from the dead. Sunrise services were held because Nimrod/Saturn was the sun god. Easter rabbits and eggs, among other customs. All this practiced long before Jesus was born or died on the cross, which even before then the Lord embraced as detestable, provoking, abominable. He asked Ezekiel (above), "is this a trivial matter . . . ?"

Feasting, drunkenness, orgies, frenzied and out of control dancing, sacrificing children were all involved in worshiping Asherah and Baal (which means lord). Cult prostitution was practiced in the worship of Asherah. The temple eunuchs castrated themselves and dressed as women as a form of worship to Asherah.

These were the ways of Jezebel and the practices she brought to the northern kingdom of Israel, which king Ahab promoted. Jezebel was known as a liar, adulterer, and murderer. It is the mixing of these spiritual adulteries and abominable practices which celebrated and worshiped the Devil, demons, and the demigods or giants that the Lord detests. It was the ruin of Israel and Judah. Now through the Romans, the sixth kingdom of the beast who have the same practices worshiping the same gods, the Church is being seduced. The Nicolaitans were a major example of those who were guilty of this. This was a problem to contend with even while the Apostles were alive. Both Jude and Peter harshly addressed those involved with these tendencies.

Although Jesus is speaking to the church of Thyatira and their issues we are, however, examining what the Lord is revealing about the fourth Church age concerning His Church as a whole.

The Fourth Church Age

For: *"I know your works, your love, faith, service, patient endurance, and that your last works are more than the first."*

Against/warning:*". . .You tolerate your (that) woman Jezebel, who calls herself a prophetess. She teaches and seduces my servants to commit sexual immorality, and to eat things sacrificed to idols. 21 I gave her time to repent, but she refuses to repent of her sexual immorality."*

"I know your works, your love, faith, service, patient endurance, and that your last works are more than the first." This is the fourth Church age and along with the third, they follow the persecution by the Roman Empire in the second Church age. That age was the time of the ten time periods under ten different Roman emperors who persecuted the Church. The last one was Diocletian with his reign of terror against the Christians lasting for ten years. Diocletian was the worst. During the Great Persecution (303–313 AD) the emperor ordered Christian owned properties confiscated, buildings, churches, and the homes of Christians torn down and their sacred books collected and burned. Christians were arrested, tortured, mutilated, burned, starved, and condemned to gladiatorial contests to amuse spectators.

The first emperor in the third Church age was Constantine. In comparison, the Church has gone from the worst circumstances during the second Church age to a golden age—the third Church age. Some at the time considered it was the time of the New Jerusalem as the Church gained acceptance and even was caused to prosper by the ones who formally were their worst enemy!

Through Constantine, the Church came into power and riches, eventually sharing the rule over the people of the Roman world. He even helped reorganize the Church government. St. Constantine the Great is considered equal to the Apostles. However, Constantine teaches the ways of Balaam and the Church is seduced. He is welcomed in with open arms, even thought to be the Church's hero and savior. That was the time of the third Church age when the teachings of Balaam entered in, affecting the Church and the ways of the Nicolaitans came to be.

In the fourth Church age, 300 years after the fall of the Roman Empire on Christmas Day December 25, 800 AD, the Roman Church becomes queen Jezebel. It becomes the seventh kingdom of the beast. The elect comply and accept her rulership of the Church. Later in Revelation, Jesus calls His elect to come out of her so they avoid suffering the Church's punishment, while calling her Babylon.

". . .You tolerate your (that) woman Jezebel . . . " A new and worse error has its starting point in the third Church age, building on the error of the first (the loss of their first love), and then spilling over into the fourth age—this Church age. This new error which first entered into the third Church age, eventually consumes almost every individual Christian right up to the seventh Church age. Here is an ironic thing, the Church came out of the second Church age with a clean heart when it had been persecuted and oppressed. Nothing was found against that Church age. The third Church age is not a time of persecution or oppression but one of tolerance, acceptance, and even prosperity. However, the Church comes out of this time of prosperity corrupted. Corrupt in a way that it is the actual downfall of the Church reaching all the way to the last age. The observation was correct that Satan could not persecute into destruction. It had the opposite effect. When the one thing doesn't work he does as Balaam and seduces the Church into sinning against God and bringing destruction on themselves. ("You can catch more flies with honey than with vinegar." "If you can't beat them join them.")

Note: History shows us why it is necessary for the Lord to impose hardships and persecution on us in order to make us pure, and keep us pure. History also shows us prosperity and power in the world leads to our downfall and adulteress betrayal of God. Given this, can we really ask, "Why does God let all of these bad things happen to us?" What a sad commentary this speaks towards, what it takes to keep the human heart blameless and clean hands before God.

Jezebel (Babylon) now enters the Church. One of the trademarks of Jezebel is to elevate, do the work for, establish, even empower and enforce her Ahab. All this, while standing back behind the scenes and secretly carrying out her own agenda through her Ahab—she is the real power. Queen Jezebel was Pope Leo III and his Church. The newly revived Roman Empire was her Ahab.

On Christmas Day December 25, 800AD, Pope Leo III crowned Charlemagne the king of the Franks, emperor of the Roman Empire and "Augustus of the Romans". By this act, the fatal head wound of one of the seven heads of the beast is healed, 300 years after it had received it's death blow. Rome, the city on seven hills and the head of the Empire, had been sacked. The head of the empire is the city of Rome; the head and seat of its government and power. By this same act the Roman Church, which sits in Rome on the seven hills, now becomes the ruler of the revived Roman Empire. His revived Roman Empire was eventually called the Holy Roman Empire because of the Church's authority over it.

One of the major reasons Pope Leo III decided to revive the Roman Empire was because his position as pope became threatened. The people of Italy became disillusioned with him. Plots were made against him. A group of armed men attacked him and tried to cut out his tongue and tear out his eyes, and depose him as pope. Their reason was that he stood accused of both perjury and adultery. Take out his tongue, and he could no longer lie. Tear out his eyes, and he could no longer lust. Although he was rescued from the attack after being rendered unconscious, he had no real means of protection and enforcement of his authority as pope.

It was then that he decided the best course of action was to get the king of the Franks behind him to enforce his position and authority. After the intervention of the king protecting him, he invited Charlemagne to Rome. He then unexpectedly crowned and anointed Charlemagne, emperor of the Roman Empire and "Augustus of the Romans." This astonished Charlemagne at first. He reacted badly and was angry because by this act he realized it put the pope in authority over him. Although it gave him power over the nations, Charlemagne and his Holy Roman Empire was now the beast of burden, ridden by the pope of the Roman Catholic Church.

The Church ruled by the pope is the great prostitute who, with bit and bridle in hand, empowers herself on the back of the beast. However, Charlemagne came to accept his ordination because without force or by the sword he was made leader over lands he did not previously control. Leo's plan worked! The people of Italy backed down and accepted him to remain the pope over them—they tolerated him (Jezebel).

Lying, intrigue, deception, manipulation and adultery are a few of the main traits of Jezebel. Pope Leo III revived the kingdom of the beast and took authority over it, empowering himself with it. Leo (Queen Jezebel) gained a power over the nations through the force of a worldly kingdom. No longer was he and his church empowered by the Spirit of God. The Roman Church became Babylon, and its prophesied seventh kingdom. The leadership of the church, the Empire of the Franks, and the people simply accepted and complied with this new order of things. This is why Jesus holds against this Church age: "You tolerate that woman Jezebel who calls herself a prophetess."

That fateful day on December 25, 800 AD, is the day that the fourth Church age began. This event, and the effects it had on the future, is what distinguishes the fourth Church age (of becoming the seventh king and authority of Babylon) from the third Church age. The third Church age consisted of collaboration and amalgamation with the Roman Empire (Babylon). This is as Jesus, the One who walked among the lampstands, had foretold and warned His precious Church from falling into.

Again, the third Church age was seduced, letting in the ways of the beast, and was empowered by Babylon (the Rome Empire) through Constantine. However, the Roman Empire had died and the pope of the Roman Church, Leo III, revived it taking its seat of power over the nations and the fourth age began.

As a part of doing so, he revived the Roman governmental structure, its culture, even art, and architecture. The papal seat of the church of Rome, the Catholic Church, became the seventh head and crown of the beast. The seat of pope became the seventh king of Babylon. Rome, the city on seven hills remains the great city and the Harlot—the Roman Catholic Church, which sits upon the great city dressed in purple and crimson (the colors of the Catholic Church leadership).

The Double-edged sword:

Words that give life: *"But to you I say, to the rest who are in Thyatira, as many as don't have this teaching, who don't know what some call 'the deep things of Satan,' to you I say, I am not putting any other burden on you. Only hold on to what you have until I come. Nevertheless, hold that which you have firmly until I come. He who overcomes, and he who keeps my works to the end, to him I will give authority over the nations. He will rule them with a rod of iron, shattering them like clay pots; as I also have received of my Father: and I will give him the morning star."*

Note: Things have progressed to the point where in these seven letters Jesus is no longer talking to the whole Church but only to those in it who have kept themselves spiritually clean. Jesus talks about the *Church Corrupt* (ruled by Jezebel) making reference to them, however, it is apparent that He is directing His words towards those who are not part of the *Church Corrupt.* By inference, the *Church Corrupt* has made a choice and has sealed its fate. Additionally, the inference is that those who do not tolerate the Jezebelian Church leadership, and as a result are still part of the *Church Pure,* are the smallest percentage of the Church as a whole.

"But to you I say, to the rest who are in Thyatira, as many as don't have this teaching, who don't know what some call 'the deep things of Satan,' to you I say, I am not putting any other burden on you. Nevertheless, hold that which you have firmly until I come."

Note: Concerning the secret knowledge of the "the deep things of Satan," it stands to reason that these "deep things" were: The knowledge of Satan's antichrist and his empirical legacy of seven kingdoms, and the power granted him by God to rule the world. Including the prophetic knowledge that his sixth empire (Rome) would be revived from the dead resulting in the seventh and last kingdom. Just as the beast, Nimrod, would raise from the dead.

With Pope Leo III possessing that "secret knowledge" (along with some of his Church leadership) he betrayed God by stepping into that place of power granted the Devil and his beast. All it would take is to do what had been destined to happen. He had to be the one to raise the former Roman Empire back up to be the seventh king; gaining the kingdom of the beast as his. All he needed to do was to be the one to "heal the fatal head wound," reviving the empirical legacy of the beast.

All things considered, it is certain that given his position as pope and having that position at just the right time (after the fall of Rome), Leo saw it as his destiny to take that place. It must have been to him like a tomato ripe, red and juicy, ready to be picked. All the stars were aligned and only he was in a position to pick it—all he had to do was reach out and take it, then it was his.

By knowingly stepping into that place he sold his soul to gain the Devil's power and authority over the nations. Pope Leo III had fallen to a place of losing his power and position after having sinned against God, leaving him powerless to even protect his own life. However, he went from sinning and having God's hand against him, to becoming the authority and power over the nations, after making a deal with the Devil. The elect tolerated him doing the unimaginable. He opened up Pandora's box making the Church Babylon. The people simply lined up under the new order of things.

There were 300 bishops that attended the Council of Nicaea, and 1,500 who did not attend. However, overtime and with the passing of succeeding emperors after Constantine, those 300 eventually became the basis of the new Church government under the bishop of Rome, the pope. The Church, in the end, became married to the Roman Empire/Babylon just as Jezebel married Ahab, the king of Israel. As for the 1,500 bishops and their congregations, they either:

- Eventually assimilated under the authority of the Roman Catholic Church
- In later times they were genocide for not lining up and following the bishop of Rome, the pope and seventh king of the kingdom of the beast.
- Or they remained hidden, obscure pockets of communities declared to be heretics and under the threat of persecution.

It is these (the nonconformists) who Jesus is saying He will not require more from, only they must hold on to what they have (are). However, to hang on to what they had until Jesus returns, proves to be more difficult a task than it was for the second Church age. The Roman Empire, once again, started persecuting, killing, and torturing the Church. Only this time it is the Holy Roman Empire under the direction of the Church. In comparison, the second Church age was insignificant alongside the numbers and suffering perpetrated against the *Church Pure* by the *Church Corrupt.*

Below is an article giving some insight how the Roman Catholic Church and her Holy Roman Empire persecutes the remaining *Church Pure*, those who Jesus said of:

WEB Rev 2:24-29 *. . . I am not putting any other burden on you. Only hold on to what you have until I come. Nevertheless, hold that which you have firmly until I come. He who overcomes, and he who keeps my works to the end, to him I will give authority over the nations. He will rule them with a rod of iron, shattering them like clay pots; as I also have received of my Father: and I will give him the morning star.*

Jesus is referring to the time of His 1,000 year reign when He gives them that "authority over the nations." However, until then let us look at what they were up against:

Secret History of Papal Rome

The majority of people today, including Roman Catholics do not know about the true bloody history of the Papal Church of Rome. The true history of the Roman Catholic Church has been hidden away from the eyes of the masses, through the re-writing of the history books, so that they cannot see the truth about the antichrist church, otherwise known as Babylon, the mother of Harlots. But on this page we will give you a glimpse into the history of Papal Rome, with a timeline of events that took place during the past 1000 years.

Further down the page you will see quotes from the few available (if you dig deep) history books revealing the truth about Papal persecutions.

Please know, this is not out of hate for the people WITHIN the Catholic Church, but hate for what the Catholic Church has done and for what she CONTINUES to do. God is calling His precious children OUT of this church (Babylon) and we are here to help sound that call!

"Under the guise of Christianity, the Papal Church committed more enormities than ever disgraced the annals of paganism. Disregarding the maxims and the spirit of the Gospel, the papal Church, arming herself with the power of the sword, vexed the Church of God and wasted it for several centuries, a period most appropriately termed in history, the 'dark ages'. "The kings of the earth, gave their power to the Beast." (Fox's Book of Martyrs, Ch. IV)

"Roman Catholicism was born in blood, has wallowed in blood, and has quenched its thirst in blood, and it is in letters of blood that its true history is written." (Baron DePonnat, 1940)

"I learned much from the Order of the Jesuits, said Hitler ... Until now, there has never been anything more grandiose, on the earth, than the hierarchical organization of the Catholic Church. I transferred much of this organization into my own party." (Hermann Rauschning, former national-socialist chief of the government of Dantzig: 'Hitler m'a dit', (Ed. Co-operation, Paris 1939, pp.266, 267, 273 ss).

"And I saw the woman drunken with the blood of the saints, and with the blood of the martyrs of Jesus." (Revelation 17:6)

The following are just a few examples of Papal crimes

1209 - The Albigensian Crusades in southern France. Roman Catholic crusaders slaughter approximately 20,000 citizens of Beziers, France on July 22, 1209. Both Albigensian Christians and Catholics were slain. By the time the Roman Catholic armies finished their crusade, almost the entire population of southern France (mostly Albigensian Christians) has been exterminated.

1236 - Roman Catholic crusaders slaughter Jews in the Anjou and Poitou regions of western France in a severe wave of persecution.

1481 - - At the direction of the Roman Catholic inquisitors, authorities torture, burn and slaughter tens, even hundreds of thousands of people during the Spanish Inquisition (Jean Antoine Llorentine, History of the Inquistion; as cited in R.W. Thompson, The Papacy and the Civil Power (New York, 1876); as cited in Dave Hunt, A Woman Rides the Beast).

1540 - 1570 - Roman Catholic armies butcher at least 900,000 Waldensian Christians of all ages during this 30-year period (source: Halley's Bible Handbook).

1553 - 1558 - Roman Catholic Queen Mary I of England (aka bloody Mary) attempts to bring England back under the yoke of papal tyranny. During her reign, nearly 300 men and woman are burned to death at the sake. Her victims include bishops, scholars, and other Protestant leaders.

1572 - St. Bartholomew's Day Massacre. French Roman Catholic soldiers begin killing Protestants in Paris on the night of August 24, 1572. The soldiers kill at least 10,000 Protestants during the first three days. At least 8000 more Protestants are killed as the slaughter spreads to the countryside.

1618 - 1648 - The Thirty Years War. This bloody, religious war is planned, instigated, and orchestrated by the Roman Catholic Jesuit order and its agents in an attempt to exterminate all the Protestants in Europe. Many countries in central Europe lose up to half their population (see Cushing B. Hassell, History of the Church of God, Chapter XVII).

1641 - 1649 - Eight years of Jesuit-instigated Roman Catholic butchery of Irish Protestants claims the lives of hundreds of thousands of Protestants (see Cushing B. Hassell, History of the Church of God, Chapter XVII).

1685 - French Roman Catholic soldiers slaughter approximately 500,000 French Protestant Huguenots on the orders of Roman Catholic King Louis 14 of France.

1941 - 1945 - The Roman Catholic Ustashi in Yugoslavia butchered Hundreds of thousands of Yugoslav citizens, Serbs, Jews and Roma. And Hundreds of thousands were forced to convert to Catholicism.

1949 - 1953 - With the support from the Columbian government, the Roman Catholic Church had 60,000 Protestants and non-Catholics shot, drowned and emasculated. Pope Pius XII awarded the Columbian President with one of the highest awards the church can give.

During her full reign of terror, the Papacy had caused the cruel death of at least 50 MILLION people. The following are quotes from the few available history books concerning Papal persecutions.

"Bertrand, the Papal Legate, wrote a letter to Pope Honorius, desiring to be recalled from the croisade against the primitive witnesses and contenders for the faith. In that authentic document, he stated, that within fifteen years, 300,000 of those crossed soldiers had become victims to their own fanatical and blind fury. Their unrelenting and insatiable thirst for Christian and human blood spared none within the reach of their impetuous despotism and unrestricted usurpations. On the river Garonne, a conflict occurred between the croisaders, with their ecclesiastical leaders, the Prelates of Thoulouse and Comminges; who solemnly promised to all their vassals the full pardon of sin, and the possession of heaven immediately, if they were slain in the battle. The Spanish monarch and his confederates acknowledged that they must have lost 400,000 men, in that tremendous conflict, and immediately after it-but the Papists boasted, that including the women and children, they had massacred more than two millions of the human family, in that solitary croisade against the southwest part of France." (Bourne, George, The American Textbook of Popery, Griffith & Simon, Philadelphia, 1846, pp. 402-403)

"The Catholic crusade against the Albigenses in Southern France (from 1209-1229), under Popes Innocent III., Honorius III. and Gregory IX., was one of the bloodiest tragedies in human history ... The number of Albigenses that perished in the twenty years war is estimated at from one to two millions." (Cushing B. Hassell, History of the Church of God, Chapter XIV)

"Need I speak to you of the thirty years war in Germany, which was mainly instigated by the Jesuits, in order to deprive the Protestants of the right of free religious worship, secured to them by the treaty of Augsburg? Or of the Irish rebellion, of the inhuman butchery of about fifteen millions of Indians in South America, Mexico and Cuba, by the Spanish papists? In short, it is calculated by authentic historians, that papal Rome has shed the blood of sixty-eight millions of the human race in order to establish her unfounded claims to religious dominion." (The Glorious Reformation by S. S. SCHMUCKER, 1838 -- citing Dr. Brownlee's 'Popery an enemy to civil liberty', p. 105)

"This was the century of the last religious wars in Christendom, the Thirty Years War in Germany, fomented by the Jesuits, reducing the people to cannibalism, and the population of Bohemia from 4,000,000 to 780,000, and of Germany from 20,000,000 to 7,000,000, and making Southern Germany almost a desert." (Cushing B. Hassell, History of the Church of God, Chapter XVII)

"In one word, the church of Rome has spent immense treasures and shed, in murder, the blood of sixty eight millions and five hundred thousand of the human race, to establish before the astonished and disgusted world, her fixed determination to annihilate every claim set up by the human family to liberty, and the right of unbounded freedom of conscience." (W C Brownlee, Popery an enemy to civil liberty, 1836, pp. 104-105)

"There perished under pope Julian 200,000 Christians: and by the French massacre, on a moderate calculation, in 3 months, 100,000. Of the Waldenses there perished 150,000; of the Albigenses, 150,000. There perished by the Jesuits in 30 years only 900,000. The Duke of Alva destroyed by the common hangman alone, 36,000 persons; the amount murdered by him is set down by Grotius at 100,000! There perished by the fire, and tortures of the Inquisition in Spain, Italy, and France 150,000 ... In the Irish massacres there perished 150,000 Protestants! To sum up the whole, the Roman Catholic church has caused the ruin, and destruction of a

million and a half of Moors in Spain; nearly two millions of Jews South America in Europe. In Mexico, and , including the islands of Cuba and St. Domingo, fifteen millions of Indians, in 40 years, fell victims to popery. And in Europe, and the East Indies, and in America, 50 millions of Protestants, at least, have been murdered by it! Thus the church of Rome stands before the world, 'the woman in scarlet, on the scarlet colored Beast.' A church claiming to be Christian, drenched in the blood of sixty-eight millions, and five hundred thousand human beings!' (W. C. Brownlee, Letters in the Roman Catholic controversy, 1834, pp. 347-348)

"Alexander Campbell, well known religions leader of the nineteenth century, stated in debate with John B. Purcell, Bishop of Cincinnati, in 1837 that the records of historians and martyrologists show that it may be reasonable to estimate that from fifty to sixty-eight millions of human beings died, suffered torture, lost their possessions, or were otherwise devoured by the Roman Catholic Church during the awful years of the Inquisition. Bishop Purcell made little effort to refute these figures." (Citing A Debate on the Roman Catholic Religion, Christian Publishing Co., 1837, p. 327.) ... (The Shadow of Rome, by John B. Wilder; Zondervan Publishing Co., 1960, page 87)

"Let us keep a sense of proportion. The record of 'Christianity' [Roman Catholic] from the days when it first obtained the power to persecute is one of the most ghastly in history. The total number of Manichaeans, Arians, Priscillianists, Paulicians, Bogomiles, Cathari, Waldensians, Albigensians, witches, Lollards, Hussites, Jews and Protestants killed because of their rebellion against Rome clearly runs to many millions; and beyond these actual executions or massacres is the enormously larger number of those who were tortured, imprisoned, or beggared. I am concerned rather with the positive historical aspect of this. In almost every century a large part of the race has endeavored to reject the Christian religion, and, if in those centuries there had been the same freedom as we enjoy, Roman Catholicism would, in spite of the universal ignorance, have shrunk long ago into a sect. The religious history of Europe has never yet been written." (The Story Of Religious Controversy Chapter XXIII by Joseph McCabe (an atheist) who lived from 1867 to 1955)

"Mede has calculated from good authorities 'that in the war with the Albigenses and Waldenses there perished of these people, in France alone, 1,000,000.'" (Christ and Antichrist, by Samuel J. Cassels, 1846, page 257)

"Who have their dungeon cells under their cathedrals, in which they claim, as inquisitors of their own diocese, to imprison free men in our republic? Foreign popish bishops! And the facts respecting a man being so confined and scourged, in the cells at Baltimore [AMERICA], until he recanted, have been published, and not to this day contradicted! ... Who are in the habit of uttering ferocious threats to assassinate and burn up those Protestants who successfully oppose Romanism? The foreign papists! I have in my possession the evidence of no less than six such inhuman threatenings against myself." (W. C. Brownlee, Popery the Enemy of Civil and Religious Liberty, J. S. Taylor, New York, 1836, p.210-211)

"It is reckoned that during the reign of Justinian, Africa lost five millions of inhabitants; thus Arianism was extinguished in that region, not by any enforcement of conformity, but by the extermination of the race which had introduced and professed it. - History of the Christian Church, J.C. Robertson, Vol. 1, p. 521." (Bunch, Taylor, The Book of Daniel, p. 101)

[footnote, speaking of Pope Innocent VIII] "Yet on the papal throne he played the zealot against the Germans, whom he accused of magic, in his bull Summis desiderantes affectibus, etc., and also against the Hussites, whom he well nigh exterminated." (Williams, Henry Smith, The Historian's History of the World, vol. 8, p. 643)

"The inquisitor Reinerius, who died in 1259, has left it on record: 'Concerning the sects of ancient heretics, observe, that there have been more than seventy: all of which, except the sects of the Manichaeans and the Arians and the Runcarians and the Leonists which have infected Germany, have through the favour of God, been destroyed." (Broadbent, E.H., The Pilgrim Church, Gospel Folio Press, 2002, p. 90 (originally published in 1931)

"An edict was issued under the regency of Theodora, which decreed that the Paulicians should be exterminated by fire and sword, or brought back to the Greek church ... It is affirmed by civil and ecclesiastical historians, that, in a short reign, one hundred thousand Paulicians were put to death." (Andrew Miller, Short Papers on Church, London, Chapter 16)

"The whole number of victims who have been offered up in Europe since the beginning of the Reformation? Partly by war, partly by the Inquisition, and a thousand other methods of Romish cruelty? No less within forty years, if the computation of an eminent writer be just, than five and forty millions!" (John Wesley, 'Doctrine of Original Sin', Part I, section II.8, 1757, Wesley's Works, edited by Thomas Jackson, vol. 9, pp. 217-19)

"The inquisition, which was established in the twelfth century against the Waldenses ... was now more effectually set to work. Terrible persecutions were carried on in various parts of Germany, and even in Bohemia, which continued about thirty years, and the blood of the saints was said to flow like rivers of water. The countries of Poland, Lithuania, and Hungary, were in a similar manner deluged with Protestant blood." (Buck, Charles, A Theological Dictionary, containing Definitions of All Religious Terms; ..., Philadelphia, Thomas Cowperthwait & Co., 1838, article 'Persecution')

"Those who were not put to death suffered imprisonment, had their houses pulled down, their lands laid waste, their property stolen, and their wives and daughters, after being ravished, sent into convents ... If any fled from these cruelties, they were pursued through the woods, hunted and shot like wild beasts...At the head of the dragoons, in all the provinces of France, marched the bishops, priests, friars, &c. the clergy being ordered to keep up the cruel spirit of the military. An order was published for demolishing all protestant churches." (Southwell, Henry, The new book of martyrs; or complete Christian martyrology. Containing an authentic and genuine historical account of the many dreadful persecutions against the Church of Christ, in all parts of the world, ... Imprint London : printed for J. Cooke, [1765?] page 108-109)

"In Bohemia, by 1600, in a population of 4,000,000, 80 per cent were Protestant. When the Hapsburgs and Jesuits had done their work, 800,000 were left, all Catholics ... In Austria and Hungary half the population Protestant, but under the Hapsburgs and Jesuits they were slaughtered ... In Poland, by the end of the 16th century, it seemed as if Romanism was about to be entirely swept away, but here too, the Jesuits, by persecution, killed Reform. In Italy, the

Pope's own country, the Reformation was getting a real hold; but the Inquisition got busy, and hardly a trace of Protestantism was left." (Halley's Bible Handbook, p.798)

"The Horrors of the Inquisition, ordered and maintained by the Popes, over a period of 500 years, in which unnumbered millions were Tortured and Burned, constitute the MOST BRUTAL, BEASTLY, and DEVILISH PICTURE in all history." (Halley's Bible Handbook, p.732)

6,000+ Catholic priests abused 16,000+ (known) children since 1950 in America

500,000 children taken from families, forced into Catholic institutions and abused in Australia from 1930 to 1970

4,000+ children sexually abused in Australia since 1980

Hundreds of thousands of children abused in Catholic and Protestant 'care homes' in Germany between 1950 to 1970

Pope John Paul II ignored the abuse of 2,000 boys in Austria over decades and covered up 'innumerable' cases of abuse

700,000+ men women and children in Croatia tortured and killed by Catholic Church in 1940's

20,000+ children abused by Catholic Church since 1945 in Netherlands

100,000+ children abused and killed in government and Catholic institutions in Canada from 1930 to 1980

1,700+ Catholic priests accused of abuse in Brazil

Catholic Church sends paedophile priests to South American churches

Tens of thousands of children abused by Catholic priests in Ireland between 1930 to 1990

10,000+ women abused in Catholic institutions in Ireland between 1920 to 1996

Hundreds of Catholic priests abused children in the Philippines between 1980 to 2000

800,000 people massacred in Rwanda, with support from Catholic Church in 1994

Thousands of children and adults abused in Catholic 'care homes' in Scotland in the 60's and 70's

300,000 babies stolen from mothers by Catholic Church in Spain between 1930 - 1990

Thousands of children tortured and abused in Catholic schools in Switzerland between 1930 to 1970

Friends, please open your eyes to this antichrist church. This is not God's church whatsoever. It is an apostate church and history PROVES her status as the main Bible 'antichrist' system. The pope thinks he sits IN PLACE OF Christ, acting as if he is God, which is what antichrist actually means in the original language. Someone who puts himself IN PLACE OF Christ. And the doctrines of this church are an abomination to our Holy Heavenly Father. Heed the call today! COME OUT OF HER MY PEOPLE! (Revelation 18:4).[12]

The words that give judgment: *"Behold, I will throw her into a bed, and those who commit adultery with her into great oppression, unless they repent of her works. [23] I will kill her children with Death, and all the assemblies* (churches) *will know that I am he who searches the minds and hearts. I will give to each one of you according to your deeds."*

Keeping in mind Jesus is talking to the Church—all churches of all ages. Right here He says He is going to bring judgment to the whole Church who has let Jezebel (Babylon) into it and continues to tolerate her. And to all those who committed spiritual adultery with her and to every generation after of the *Church Corrupt.* This includes both churches of the western and eastern empires.

The Lord's warning that He had given time to repent and that He would strike her to a bed of suffering, and strike her children dead, had its fulfillment through the spread of the Bubonic Plague. It wiped out an estimated 50% to 60% of the population of Europe, the western Church and 40% of the region of Constantinople, the eastern Church. The plague had its peak in the years 1348-1350 AD. It took Europe 150 years to recover the population it lost in the plague. It's interesting to note that the plague came first to Italy and then spread to France and then the rest of Europe. The Church of Rome and the nation of France both created the Holy Roman Empire.

The characteristics of His person to this church: *"The Son of God, who has his eyes like a flame of fire, and his feet are like burnished brass* (bronze), *says these things"*

Jesus identifies Himself as the "Son of God." By doing so He is not only making clear that He has a right because the Church is His Bride, but that He also has the authority to back His words. When in his vision, John beheld the great prostitute and saw what was to become of the Church, he was "astonished." He was in awe and wonder. The angel had to explain to John how this could be. He had to console John by explaining the mystery of how this transformation could and would happen—the Church becoming Babylon. The offspring of Eve, in the end, becomes the offspring of the Devil (who hates and is in a state of enmity with Eve and her (true) line of offspring).

Jesus tells us He has eyes like "a flame of fire." He does not see from reflective light as we do. That is when light hits an object and illuminates it by bouncing off and reflecting it into our eyes. Not so, for Jesus the Son of God. When He looks at something His eyes bring a thing to light. The light from His eyes of flaming fire expose and illuminate whatever He looks at. Nothing He looks at can remain hidden, a mystery, or in the dark.

NLT Heb 4:12 For the word of God is full of living power. It is sharper than the sharpest knife, cutting deep into our innermost thoughts and desires. It exposes us for what we really are.
NLT Heb 4:13 Nothing in all creation can hide from him. Everything is naked and exposed before his eyes. This is the God to whom we must explain all that we have done.

Even in our day after the Church of Rome has shown its true colors, we too are astonished. It is nearly impossible to accept the reality of what the Church has turned into. Like John we almost must believe the Church is the bride of Christ, but the truth is that since Christmas Day December 25, 800 AD, His beloved Church became Babylon, its seventh kingdom, and no longer His bride.

NIV Rev 17:15 Then the angel said to me, "The waters you saw, where the prostitute sits, are peoples, multitudes, nations and languages.
NIV Rev 17:16 The beast and the ten horns you saw (that she rides and controls with bridle and bit in his mouth) will hate the prostitute (the Church Corrupt). They will bring her to ruin and leave her naked; they will eat her flesh and burn her with fire.
NIV Rev 17:17 For God has put it into their hearts to accomplish his purpose by agreeing to give the beast their power to rule, until God's words are fulfilled.
NIV Rev 17:18 The woman (the Roman Catholic Church) you saw is the great city (Rome) that rules over the kings of the earth."

It should not escape us that in our contemporary times, even the Church who struggled to attain reformation has for the most part failed. As the dust they stirred up has settled, they too have become the very thing they hated in the Catholic Church.

Notes

[12] *Secret History of Papal Rome* (n.d.). Retrieved December 2017, from End Times Prophecy: http://www.end-times-prophecy.org/secret-history-catholic-church.html

CHAPTER 8

Sardis

The Fifth Church Age

To the Church in Sardis

NLT Rev 3:1 *"Write this letter to the angel of the church in Sardis. This is the message from the one who has the sevenfold Spirit of God and the seven stars: "I know all the things you do, and that you have a reputation for being alive—but you are dead.*

NLT Rev 3:2 *Now wake up! Strengthen what little remains, for even what is left is at the point of death. Your deeds are far from right in the sight of God.*

NLT Rev 3:3 *Go back to what you heard and believed at first; hold to it firmly and turn to me again* (repent!). *Unless you do, I will come upon you suddenly, as unexpected as a thief.*

NLT Rev 3:4 *"Yet even in Sardis there are some who have not soiled their garments with evil deeds. They will walk with me in white, for they are worthy.*

NLT Rev 3:5 *All who are victorious will be clothed in white. I will never erase their names from the Book of Life, but I will announce before my Father and his angels that they are mine.*

NLT Rev 3:6 *Anyone who is willing to hear should listen to the Spirit and understand what the Spirit is saying to the churches.*

The Fifth Church Age

For: None *"... Your deeds are far from right in the sight of God."*

Against: *"... you have a reputation for being alive—but you are dead.*

The Church is dead spiritually to Jesus and they don't even know it. The Church thinks itself to be alive and well serving Jesus while carrying on business as usual, in spite of all the challenges it faces in trying to pick up the pieces after the Black (Bubonic) Plague. They do not even realize after all this, that they have separated themselves from their union with the Lord and are instead married to the beast, serving the Devil. They are ignorant that they have become the seventh kingdom of the beast—or are they?

The Lord had warned in the age before this, that He had given Jezebel time to repent and she refused. As such, He would put her children on a bed of suffering and kill them. He was true to His warning and came against them! The world was decimated, however, the Roman Church and the Eastern Church of Constantinople (which is the creation of Constantine) still has not gotten the message. Jesus says that what little is left is at the point of death. However, the Roman Church is alive and well and enjoys dominance over all the nations of the earth, including the hearts and souls of the people in it. He continues by pointing out that their deeds are far from being right or righteous in the eyes of God! Jesus reminds them so they would not be deluded concerning what they had just been through and why it happened to them. This is so they would know that something needs to change. However, the Church has not repented or corrected its ways of empowering itself with the Holy Roman Empire and lording over the nations. The fifth Church age begins in the aftermath of the Black Plague around 1400 AD.

A Distant Mirror

Barbara Tuchman's book, *A Distant Mirror*, reflects on the Black Death. The descriptions she supplies are taken from the writings of the time. Even if one makes allowances for exaggerations, it is so awful that it defies the imagination. Below is part of that account.

There were many to echo the account of inhumanity and few to balance it, for the plague was not the kind of calamity that inspired mutual health. Its loatheness and deadliness did not herd people together in mutual distress, but only prompted their desire to escape each other.

A Franciscan friar in Sicily stated: Magistrates and notaries refused to come and make out the wills of the dying. What was worse, even the priests did not come to hear their confessions or hear last rites. A clerk of the Archbishop of Canterbury reported the same of English priests who turned away from the care of their children in the church because of fear of death.

Cases of parents deserting children, and children deserting parents were reported across Europe from Scotland to Russia. The calamity chilled the hearts of man, wrote Boccaccio in his famous account of the plague in Florence that serves as the introduction to the Decameron. One man shunned another; kinsfolk held aloof;

brother was forsaken by brother; husband by wife. Nay, what is more and scarcely to be believed, mothers and fathers were found to abandon their own children to their fate, untended, alone, unvisited, as if they had been strangers.

Exaggeration and literary pessimism are common in the 14th century, but the Pope's position was as a sober careful observer who reported the same phenomena: "A father did not visit his son, nor did a son visit his father. Charity was dead."

That effect upon Europe created a lasting effect, because the plague bankrupted Christianity. In its moment of trial, the Christian religion failed. Faced with this disaster, the veneer of civilization and religion disappeared. It is that failure that helped bring about after the plague the Renaissance and the Reformation – both events marking where the modern world begins.[13]

The end of the Black Plague is the end of the fourth Church age, and it begins the fifth Church age. As described in "A Distant Mirror," the Church failed and thereby was as Jesus says, dead. They still held their position and power in the world as an organization, however, the magical hold they had over the hearts and souls of the people was now crumbling. ". . . you have a reputation for being alive—but you are dead." Jesus of course means this spiritually.

However, what that looks like in worldly life is that He had just purged the Church breaking its spell of power over the people of the earth through the Black Plague. The people were indeed disillusioned, as Barbara Tuchman described. The Lord needed people to question their relationship with God and their faith in the pope. Then get back to how it was in the beginning. Meaning, the way things were before the New Covenant relationship became a twisted parody of what it once was. By what He did in the fourth Church age through the Black Plague, the Lord was setting the stage for a return to what things once were.

The Church as an organization still had its place and position but because of the widespread disillusionment in the failures of the Church, people began to look elsewhere other than to the pope or the Church for answers. Some turned to science and reason and began the Renaissance. Others continued to look to God, however, in their disillusionment Christianity began to leave the Church, no longer idolizing the pope. As a result, this sparked the Reformation.

Yes, the Church still had worldly power and authority, however, it was dead and an exodus began to come out of her. The fourth Church age has its end with the promised judgment of Jesus, the Black Plague. The fifth Church age has its beginning with the end of the Black Plague and an exodus out of the Church (who Jesus calls "dead" to Him). This exodus is commonly referred to as, the Protestant Reformation.

Note: The worldly *Church Corrupt*, including the Roman Catholic Church along with the eastern or Greek Church of Constantinople, will have its total and global annihilation during the great tribulation. It will never rise from the ashes of its destruction ever again.

Warning: *"Now wake up! Strengthen what little remains, for even what is left is at the point of death. Your deeds are far from right in the sight of God."*

The Cup of the LORD'S Wrath

NIV Isa 51:17 Awake, awake! Rise up, O Jerusalem, you who have drunk from the hand of the LORD the cup of his wrath, you who have drained to its dregs the goblet that makes men stagger.
NIV Isa 51:18 Of all the sons she bore there was none to guide her; of all the sons she reared there was none to take her by the hand.
NIV Isa 51:19 These double calamities have come upon you—who can comfort you?—ruin and destruction, famine and sword—who can console you?
NIV Isa 51:20 Your sons have fainted; they lie at the head of every street, like antelope caught in a net. They are filled with the wrath of the LORD and the rebuke of your God.
NIV Isa 51:21 Therefore hear this, you afflicted one, made drunk, but not with wine.
NIV Isa 51:22 This is what your Sovereign LORD says, your God, who defends his people: "See, I have taken out of your hand the cup that made you stagger; from that cup, the goblet of my wrath, you will never drink again.
NIV Isa 51:23 I will put it into the hands of your tormentors, who said to you, 'Fall prostrate that we may walk over you.' And you made your back like the ground, like a street to be walked over."
NIV Isa 52:1 Awake, awake, O Zion, clothe yourself with strength. Put on your garments of splendor . . .

This fifth Church age is a "wake up" call from the Lord to strengthen what little remains before it is too late—before it dies completely. This fifth Church age is a call for the messengers and prophets of God to arise and bring the people out of her (the *Church Corrupt*) and into the *Church Pure*. The fifth Church age is the age of the

Reformation. Life as people knew it, ceased. It is a time to pick up the pieces. It is a time to rebuild, rethink, and reform. The Lord says to this Church age: "Go back to what you heard and believed at first; hold to it firmly and turn to me again."

NIV Ecc 3:1 There is a time for everything, and a season for every activity under heaven:

NIV Ecc 3:2 a time to be born and a time to die, a time to plant and a time to uproot,

NIV Ecc 3:3 a time to kill and a time to heal, a time to tear down and a time to build,

NIV Ecc 3:4 a time to weep and a time to laugh, a time to mourn and a time to dance,

NIV Ecc 3:5 a time to scatter stones and a time to gather them, a time to embrace and a time to refrain,

NIV Ecc 3:6 a time to search and a time to give up, a time to keep and a time to throw away,

NIV Ecc 3:7 a time to tear and a time to mend, a time to be silent and a time to speak,

NIV Ecc 3:8 a time to love and a time to hate, a time for war and a time for peace.

The fourth Church age was a time of tearing down and uprooting. This fifth Church age is a fresh opportunity—a time to heal, to rebuild, a time to search, and a time to speak. There was no chance to change the direction things were going in, however, now that things are torn down, Jesus is raising up prophets ("voices") in the land; so they would not rebuild that same old barn that just got torn down (as they say). The hearts and souls of the people are ripe for change. They are ready to search and find out what went wrong, and how to get back to the beginning. They were ripe for going back to first-century values and finding out what they were.

The Double-edged sword:

Words that give life: *". . . in Sardis* (in the fifth Church age) *there are some who have not soiled their garments with evil deeds. They will walk with me in white, for they are worthy. All who are victorious will be clothed in white* (they will receive a celestial [white] body and be with Me where I am). *I will never erase their names from the Book of Life, but I will announce before my Father and his angels that they are mine."*

In this Church age Jesus says there are "some who . . ." in other translations it says appropriately, "Yet you (still) have "<u>a few people</u>" in Sardis (the fifth Church age) who have not soiled their clothes. Note that in the previous Church age it has gone from the "rest of you," to the *Church Pure* dwindling down to what Jesus calls, "a few people." This whole calamity started with 300 out of 1,800 worldwide bishops and all their congregations being seduced down to "a few people" in this age. There are FEW people left in this age that are His body.

Most likely, the majority of the "few" are hidden away with the monastics in the caves and in the deserts. Perhaps it is in small but secret groups, or individuals among the church congregations, who truly follow the Spirit through their own conscience. In this Church age comes the voices who call us out of the Church beginning the Protestant Reformation. The Lord is looking for numbers to be added to the "few". Those who abandon the Church do so in order to return to what was first taught when Jesus walked the earth. Again, these few and the voices which sprung from them, are what ushers in the beginning of the fifth Church age.

A couple of the voices or prophets who were at the beginning of this Church age were John Wycliffe and John Huss around 1517 AD. Then later were voices like Luther, and Calvin. Some of the voices of this Church age took the sacred Scriptures (the Bible) and translated them into the common languages giving access to the common people. However, the Roman Church and the kings of the world were blind to what Jesus warned them about in these very letters. They wanted to recapture their greatness and power, even capitalize on the times. They would not give up their power and greatness so easily!

It would be in perilous times that the Church reformers did their work constantly risking life and limb. The Roman Church and the kings she committed adultery with, tortured and killed the "few" in the most cruel ways. They did the same to those who followed them killing tens of millions. Truly the darnel the Devil planted in Jesus' wheat field did not want His wheat to survive any more than Cain wanted Abel to remain. This is why Jesus said (looking forward from John's day when He was walking among the lampstands) to these few who risked their lives against the *Church Corrupt*:

WEB Rev 3:5 "*He who overcomes will be arrayed in white garments, and I will in no way blot his name out of the book of life, and I will confess his name before my Father, and before his angels.*"

Those who repent will become like the few that are left. Those who overcome are the Church reformers and those who follow them breaking free from the *Church Corrupt*. It is the fifth angel of the church of Sardis, the fifth star in Jesus' hand who inspired and empowered those voices who broke free from the Church. To again name a few: John Wycliffe, John Huss, Martin Luther, John Calvin, and John Wesley.

The words that give judgment: *". . . If therefore you won't watch* (don't wake up), *I will come as a thief, and you won't know what hour I will come upon you."*

Here is a disheartening note to point out in this place of the study in regards to the Lord inspiring this message to be released to His Church: At one point while receiving this message, the Lord told me in a dream to not give this teaching to the Church because they do not want to know and are not interested. Then the angel Gabriel came to our house to pack away and seal it up for another time. In still yet another dream, Colleen was about to give birth but the doctor walked away. We chased after the doctor and could not find her. The child Colleen was to give birth to symbolizes this message. The doctor symbolizes the Holy Spirit who was no longer willing to let this message be delivered.

At the start of this study we showed that those God is giving judgment against will not be interested in what will take place and like in the days of Noah, judgment will befall them even as they go about their business.

In the first-century, Christians were well versed concerning all that happens in the end times. It was common knowledge what the Apostles taught in the first-century outlining the end times. The Church had been prepared. Even in this book of Revelation that John wrote, He said that absolutely everyone alive and dead from the beginning of time will be astonished except for those whose name which have been written in the Lamb's book of life. However, during this present age that which was common knowledge then, is as much a mystery to the Church as it is to the world. Proof of this is that there are so many different models of interpretation of Revelation. Out of them there is nothing reliable that even sounds accurate in its understanding, or has continuity or context which holds true throughout the book of Revelation, let alone the whole Bible.

The Church is focused on life in the world as much as the people in the world. They are ready for nothing as the world is. Jesus' words to the Church have come true! Most church sermons are about how to get along in life being a part of the world, and having "balance" between your worldly and spiritual life. However, James tells us:

WEB *Jas 4:4* *You adulterers and adulteresses, don't you know that friendship with the world is hostility toward God? Whoever therefore wants to be a friend of the world makes himself an enemy of God.*

Jesus is talking to the Church in these letters! He is now saying He will come up against us, the Church! He is saying to us who once knew, that like the world, He will come to us now like a thief ! We will be astonished and it will take us unaware! This is not how it was meant to be. Listen to what Paul assumes:

WEB *1Th 5:4* *But you, brothers, aren't in darkness, that the day should overtake you like a thief.*

The characteristics of His person to this church: *"This is the message from the one who has the sevenfold Spirit of God and the seven stars."*

By what Jesus says here, again, we can verify the Church age He is speaking to. He reminds them He holds the seven stars which are the angels and the prophetic voices of the seven Church ages. He reminds us that His Spirit is behind the reformer's voices that are calling His people out of the Church and back to first-century values. He told us we have to "wake up!" He is telling us by the characteristics of His person, that it is He who is sending the prophetic voices of the Reformation. It is in an effort to help us come out of her, and to believe these men and their message.

However, by speaking this in light of Him admonishing that He will come to us like a thief, He is in other words saying, "I can make that happen. All I have to do is recall those seven angels and the Church will be oblivious like the rest of the world and they will be overtaken as by a thief when I come up against them." In other words, "I can give this prophetic message to you about the future, or I can take it away from you. These stars are in the palm of My hand."

Jesus made known to the authors of this book the rest of the meaning of the message in Revelation only after much prayer and fasting. Through this message His Church can understand what the first-century Church understood and has forgotten. Therefore, because the Lord has answered prayer and has relented, it can be said with the release of the Message, as it was said in Thessalonians: We don't have to be in the dark, and we won't be surprised when He comes. Amen.

Notes

13 Wein, B. a. (n.d.). *The Black Death.* Retrieved February 2014, from JewishHistory.org: http://www.jewishhistory.org/the-black-death/

CHAPTER 9

Philadelphia

The Sixth Church Age

To the Church in Philadelphia

NAS REV 3:7 *"And to the angel of the church in Philadelphia write: He who is holy, who is true, who has the key of David, who opens and no one will shut, and who shuts and no one opens, says this:*
NAS REV 3:8 *'I know your deeds. Behold, I have put before you an open door which no one can shut, because you have a little power, and have kept My word, and have not denied My name.*
NAS REV 3:9 *'Behold, I will cause those of the synagogue of Satan, who say that they are Jews and are not, but lie—I will make them come and bow down at your feet, and make them know that I have loved you.*
NAS REV 3:10 *'Because you have kept the word of My perseverance, I also will keep you from the hour of testing, that hour which is about to come upon the whole world, to test those who dwell on the earth.*
NAS REV 3:11 *' I am coming quickly; hold fast what you have, so that no one will take your crown.*
NAS REV 3:12 *'He who overcomes, I will make him a pillar in the temple of My God, and he will not go out from it anymore; and I will write on him the name of My God, and the name of the city of My God, the new Jerusalem, which comes down out of heaven from My God, and My new name.*
NAS REV 3:13 *'He who has an ear, let him hear what the Spirit says to the churches.'*

The Quaker Church of England, starting around 1647 and leading up to establishing Philadelphia, Pennsylvania in the late 1600's, is the Church age of the Philadelphia Church (the sixth age). The Church of Philadelphia is the church this letter was written to, however, the church in Philadelphia, PA is the sixth Church age this letter is written to and about. One of the prophetic voices of the sixth age is George Fox, the founder of the Quaker Movement.

The Quakers established in Pennsylvania a territory given them by the king of England. They called their new society, which was unfettered by worldly monarchs, a "holy experiment." It was given to a Quaker by the name of William Penn as payment for a debt owed to his deceased father by king Charles II of England.

The Quakers were called Friends or the Society of Friends. However, they were also called the Quakers as a derogatory name by their detractors because while doing quiet prayer, the presence of the Holy Spirit would be so strong they would shake and quake. They were not ashamed of the label. It stuck on them.

They were a small group, they were persecuted, had little influence, and many detractors. However, God blessed their efforts, their province, Pennsylvania (which they had migrated to from England), and both their church and provincial government. Not only was the United States government designed and constructed in Philadelphia, but it was modeled after the Quaker's Church and provincial government.

We talked about the prophetic voices of the fifth Church age as being the voices of the church reformers that called us out of the *Church Corrupt*. These voices crying out for reform started more than one hundred years before Martin Luther. Long after Luther, the Church of England was born, and church reform continued to evolve over hundreds of years. Even after hundreds of years the reformers were still struggling in their own sincere ways and according to their own revelations. Their goals were the same: To rediscover the true first-century way of relating to Jesus in accordance with the New Covenant relationship.

Getting the Bible translated into many different languages around this time, and for those Bibles to get in the hands of the people, was instrumental in rediscovering first-century values. The common people were learning for themselves the teachings of both Jesus and the Apostles. However, the truth and word of God in the Bible does not read like a step by step instruction manual.

The New Testament Bible contains the teachings of Jesus and the Apostles as well as the good news of the Gospel. Additionally, in the Bible the historic acts of the Apostles are recorded, and a handful of letters written by them to different church concerns which arose while they led the Church. To truly understand the messages and the teachings of the Apostles concerning our New Covenant relationship with Christ, one must glean from what is written, and possess the aid of the Holy Spirit. That is because as stated above, there are no step by step instructions, but instead a collection of materials written by the early Church fathers. The Bible is a collection of books which give painfully accurate accounts of both acts and truths, but do not really explain the "how to's." As such, there is missing a great deal of context and foundational understanding surrounding the meanings of most of what the Bible tells us.

The Bible is rich with wisdom and instruction of how to conduct oneself in a morally good and godly way. However, it makes it difficult to fully understand what the letters, for example, may be talking about when you are only reading one side of the story. It may be clear what the Apostles are saying in response, however, without knowing exactly what they are responding to makes it really hard to give accurate context to what they say.

Add to the problems described above; the cultural differences, the meanings of colloquialisms lost over time, customs, the difference in thought paradigms, and all which is lost in translation. In spite of having the sacred Scriptures with meticulously reliable translations, all these other factors make it difficult, at best, to really get to the heart and context of the message in the Bible—what the New Covenant relationship with Christ looks like.

As detailed as the Bible is, without accurate reference points, true context, and given all the issues above, it is next to impossible to glean true and full understanding of what the Bible is saying to us.

The one corrupt universal Church (the Roman Catholic Church) buried the truth for so long keeping the Bible out of the hands of the people. This explains exactly why so many different reform churches have and still arise after hundreds of years of searching, in an effort to rediscover the true New Covenant relationship with Christ. However, the Lord commanded us in the fifth Church age to "wake up" before we completely die to Him, and remember what was lost—what we knew in the beginning. It is only with the aid and inspiration of the Holy Spirit can the truths of the Bible be revealed to us.

If we lean on our own intelligence to understand the words, we will fall short of the meanings God had in mind. If the Holy Spirit does not give us understanding of certain passages we will skew its truths. If we consider its meanings with a superficial or worldly paradigm instead of from a spiritual perspective, we will miss the mark every time. That is even if we can use the words to convey a Christian morally good message (like most of the sermons spoken these days do). This is no more obvious than in the book of Revelation. Without God granting and giving spiritual insight by His Spirit, it is impossible to understand the book of Revelation in its entirety. That is why there are so many schools of thought concerning it.

Many individuals and groups rose up in England during its civil war. In cutting to the chase, over time three groups in England became important because they had gotten the closest at rediscovering how to relate in union with Christ (according to the New Covenant relationship). These three groups were: The Puritans, the Pilgrims, and finally the Quakers who were led by George Fox. All three of these groups sought refuge and religious freedom in America.

The Puritans and the Pilgrims both came closer to first-century church values more than Luther and the other Protestants reform groups. Both Pilgrims and Puritans saw that *spiritual union* was the way to become one with Christ—to be His body and His Church. They both kept their identity tied with king and country, England.

The difference between the two groups was that one wanted to do church reform as a part of the Church of England and its monarch (from within and at the speed England reformed as a whole). The other group saw that they had to do it from outside the Church of England so they would remain pure in their revelation. Their train of thought being that it wouldn't take as long to establish true reform and then the church and country of England could follow.

Both groups came to America to have that freedom to practice and structure their societies accordingly. However, this third group, the Quakers, who settled Pennsylvania were the reformers that were the shining star that got it right. Both the Puritans and the Pilgrims who settled in America before the Quakers, persecuted them severely by imprisonment, death, mutilation including branding, burning off of the tongue with a hot poker, beatings and exile. They got the same treatment in England, however, it never stopped them from speaking out about the true condition of the Church. Also, they never resorted to fighting back or the use of violence.

In some cases they followed in the ways of Isaiah. They were known to go to places like churches and Parliament and strip-off their clothes and prophesy against them. They would also on occasion march through towns naked in a protest about the condition of the Church. They called it "being naked as a sign." They often quoted Revelation where Jesus said the Church is, ". . . poor, blind, and naked (Rev. 3:17)."

George Fox had been so disillusioned with the Church of his day that he could not bring himself to call it, "church." He called the churches "those buildings with steeples on them."

The Quakers refused to bow down to leaders, or call them lord. They simply called each other "friends." Their government was set up so that the lawmakers were subject to the laws they would institute and not be privileged in that they were above the laws. This was the case in every government on the earth. The leaders and the lawmakers were not subject to the laws imposed on the people. The way of the Quakers, believe it or not, was a new concept at that time. Their laws were very un-encumbering and allowed for individuals to be guided more by their conscience and God's Spirit. This allowed the individual the pursuit of their own ambitions as guided by the Holy Spirit.

The Quakers did not rely on taxation, but instead for all to be socially responsible. However, that being the case, private individuals made certain their city had every social benefit program a city could desire for its citizens. For example, hospitals, social welfare programs, theatres, libraries, safely constructed and clean lit streets and sidewalks, to name a few. Their city of Philadelphia and its culture was rivaled only by New York City. People from all over the world flocked to Pennsylvania and prospered because of the way their government was set up. The "holy experiment" was such a success that the U.S. government was modeled after it by the founding fathers.

The Quakers refused to use violence to enforce or protect themselves. This is one of the important reasons why the Quakers employed nudity in their protests against the Church and governments. They refused to use violence. They would instead resort to extreme behaviors to get the attention of the people and to display the seriousness of their message. They would rather do something that would indignify themselves than resort to tactics that would bring harm to others.

A good example is that although they never broke a treaty with the Indians, the French convinced the Indians they planned to. So the Indians started raiding the Quaker farms, burning them and killing all the families. In all this, they still refused to defend themselves, or to employ violence to stop them. Nor did they break their side of the agreement with the Indians.

The Quakers are famous for being the only people having anything to do with the America's who did not exploit, lie to, and break their words to the Native Americans. In fact, William Penn was given the territory of Pennsylvania to repay a debt owed to his family. He accepted it as payment, however, upon finding out that the indigenous people lived in that territory, he paid the Indians for the real estate that was given to him by the king of England.

They pioneered, prison reform, the abolishment of slavery, the underground railroad, the building of hospitals, equal rights for woman, humane treatment of the mentally ill, and many other humanitarian endeavors. This country is blessed highly by God because of the Quakers and the ideals that were taken from them to form this government.

> When the Founding Fathers met in the latter part of the 1700's to write the Constitution that would design the government of the United States, they turned to William Penn's Frame of Government for Pennsylvania. If they had turned to Puritan New England for their model there would have been an established state church. If they had turned to aristocratic Virginia for their model there would have been a privileged class. Most of the rights and freedoms that we take for granted as a

part of our way of life in America today were originally set forth in Penn's Charter of Liberties for his colony. Friends were the original architects of the free society that we enjoy.[14]

The sixth Church age is the age of the Quakers, who amazingly and unwittingly named the city which was the center of their society, "Philadelphia." George Fox and his Quakers were the zenith of church reform, returning to a first-century understanding and the New Covenant relationship with Christ. The sixth Church age began with George Fox in the mid 1600's.

The Sixth Church Age

For: *"I know that you have little power, and kept my word, and didn't deny my name."*

Against: Nothing

Warning: *"I am coming quickly! Hold firmly that which you have, so that no one takes your crown."*

It is a fair warning! One thing that the Quakers and George Fox were not, was respecters of persons. He did not bow down or even tip his hat or call authority "lord." He and other Quakers spent much time in jail not giving government authority and aristocracy the special recognition they demanded during his day. He treated everyone the same, as a friend. He did not speak in flatteries, his words were few, and truthful. He never looked for position or power, and had a humble but rock like integrity towards all that he held as true. He was a man whose first love was the Lord and he was led by the Spirit of God, as were those who followed him. Because of this, Jesus held a door open for the Quakers that no one could close on them. They did not advance using their own power to lord over men, but help men have their own relationship with the Spirit of the Lord. That is why the Lord said of them that they had little power and as such He opened doors for them that no one could close.

The Double-edged sword:

Words that give life*: "Behold, I will cause those of the synagogue of Satan, who say that they are Jews and are not, but lie—I will make them come and bow down at your feet, and make them know that I have loved you."*

At the Church of Philadelphia, this sixth letter was addressed to, they obviously had some of the same issues as the church of Smyrna. Jews who were hypocritical, believing they were superior, lying and undermining the Christians causing them to endure persecution. The way that it would relate to the sixth Church age is that the *Church Corrupt* and the governments in authority, including the other reformed churches, all mistreated the Quakers in the same way as the church of Smyrna. Jesus admonishes them to not let unjust treatment change them or cause them to bow down to the hypocrites and thereby lose their crown of glory. That at the end of it all, these pseudo-Christians who act in their own power and lord over them will be made to acknowledge who the Quakers are in Christ. The Lord will make them bow down to the Quakers—the ones who imprisoned them because they refused to bow down to their vain self-importance.

Amp Jn 7:17 If any man desires to do His will (God's pleasure), he will know (have the needed illumination to recognize, and can tell for himself) whether the teaching is from God or whether I am speaking from Myself and of My own accord and on My own authority.

Jesus is saying discernment is not dependent on knowledge or an ability to know right from wrong, or to be an expert in the Scriptures, rather it is dependent on a heart posture. To have as a preference and priority the will of God over one's own, then what seems right in that man's heart is the will of God. Conversely, what seems right to do in the man's heart who desires his own will and ambitions, will be what he personally wills, not the Lord's.

Amp Jn 7:18 He who speaks on his own authority seeks to win honor for himself. [He whose teaching originates with himself seeks his own glory.] But He Who seeks the glory and is eager for the honor of Him Who sent Him, He is true; and there is no unrighteousness or falsehood or deception in Him.

Unquestionably this was the unselfish heart of George Fox and the Quakers—eager for the honor of Him who sent them, desirous of knowing and doing only the Lord's will at the expense of their own. This is where the greatness of George Fox and his Quakers lay. They returned to their first love.

"Because you kept my command to endure, I also will keep you from the hour of testing, which is to come on the whole world, to test those who dwell on the earth." Here is the first reference of the rapture in Revelation. There are two aspects of the harvest of souls for heaven. One is the wheat and the other is the harvest of the grapes. The harvest of the wheat is the rapture, which will happen at the onset of the great tribulation. The harvest of the grapes are those made pure through the great tribulation. They are those who wash their robes in the blood of the Lamb and lose their lives because of the word of God and standing fast to their testimony.

WEB Rev 3:12 "He who overcomes, I will make him a pillar in the temple of my God, and he will go out from there no more. I will write on him the name of my God, and the name of the city of my God, the new Jerusalem, which comes down out of heaven from my God, and my own new name."

He is assuring those of the *Church Pure*, the Quakers, and those who are like-minded, that it is they who will become celestial humans, reside in the New Jerusalem and talk to Jesus face to face. It is precisely because of this standing that those who were liars and deluded themselves as greater than them, will find themselves natural humans. They will bow down before them, acknowledging the authority the celestial Quakers have over them. Jesus does not want this group to doubt themselves or how they understand the truth!

The words that give judgment: None

NIV Rev 2:4 Yet I hold this against you: You have forsaken your first love.
NIV Rev 2:5 Remember the height from which you have fallen! Repent and do the things you did at first.

NIV Rev 3:3 Remember, therefore, what you have received and heard; obey it, and repent.

The admonishment these other Church ages received, in the examples above, carried ultimatums if they failed to return to what they were first taught by Jesus, the Holy Spirit, and the Apostles. The rising up of the prophetic voices who brought reform after the Black Plague was an evolution that transpired over hundreds of years. All leading up to George Fox and the Quakers who got back to what we received and heard in the beginning. Because they truly found the height we all fell from, the sixth Church age is neither admonished by Jesus, nor told what will befall them if they do not return. By inference, this says that they indeed hit the mark. The Lord only implores them to hang on to the crown they have received by returning to their first love and the practice of true *spiritual union* with Christ. This speaks volumes about the ways of the Quakers.

The overwhelming majority of the reformed church (who did not quite hit the mark) have taken on the ways of the *Church Corrupt.* They are still struggling to know how to have a New Covenant relationship with Christ.

The characteristics of His person to this church: *"He who is holy, who is true, who has the key of David, who opens and no one will shut, and who shuts and no one opens, says this ..."*

One of the things that distinguished the Quakers as the sixth Church age is that they didn't just endure persecution because of their religious beliefs like so many others during the times of the Reformation. No, they were people who offered themselves up, both men and women, to be persecuted. This was at a time when women had no place speaking for God or speaking out against the system or the Church. Stripping away their clothes and their dignity, putting themselves in positions that they knew they would be arrested, physically mutilated, exiled, and even killed. As small as the group was compared to other reforming groups, they did this all over the world. They were so radical that even other churches that came out of the Reformation persecuted them. They did these things all to help the Church and the world to see that they were deluded and hell bound concerning their standing with God. And that the Church had become Babylon and treated their fellow man no better than the secular governments.

They were not a light hidden under a bushel, but a city on a hill whose light the whole world could see from miles away. By every account, these "Friends" returned to their first love. They lived for Jesus and every prompting He gave them. They didn't hesitate or care about how crazy the idea seemed or the effects it might have on their own person. Yes, it is these people and every Christian who takes their example of living out of love for Jesus, who will be raptured. They are who Jesus will spare the sufferings which will come upon the whole earth known as the great tribulation. This distinguishes the Quaker Church and their "holy experiment," Philadelphia, Pennsylvania as the sixth Church age.

The key of David refers to the King's keys to the great heavenly city. It is a key Jesus possesses that can unlock any door of endeavor or pursuit. Likewise, it is the key which can lock the doors from entrance of the pursuits and endeavors humans strive towards.

An interesting story in Jewish tradition is about the destruction of Jerusalem by the Romans in 70 AD. As they were sacking the city and the temple was burning down, the high priest climbed to the highest point of the temple. Seeing the lost cause of the temple, he looked up to heaven and spoke to the Lord while holding the key to the temple. Offering it up he said, if, Lord, you do not find your people worthy anymore to serve in your temple please take the key. Then a hand came out of heaven and took the key from the hand of the high priest. Here Jesus says in Rev 3:7, He has the key of David!

". . . he who opens and no one can shut, and who shuts and no one opens" The Quakers have fragmented into several factions, and there is only one of those groups who still follow the original ways of George Fox, and their numbers are few. However, the door Jesus opened with them was not shut and this is why without knowledge of them, or what they did and believed, our small church received through divine revelation the same revelation that they were given. Which is understanding what it means to be in true *spiritual union* with Christ. A union which will help avoid "the hour of trial that is going to come upon the whole world to test those who live on the earth."

The Quakers still have the same practices which surround *spiritual union* with Christ. They still have a profound love for their fellow man. Many Quaker churches, groups, and individuals are deeply driven by the foundational creed of their faith. Especially in the areas of charity and the reform of every area of life which can bring more respect towards human life, honoring the dignity of it, and easing suffering wherever it exists. They stand for and still give their human brothers freedom to follow their own conscience instead of being oppressed by laws and governments.

This is the most important thing to recognize, you can do and be and stand for all these things as a Christ follower and still lose your first love. The Quakers as a church had discovered what the first Church had lost. Given the letters written by the Apostles in the Bible, losing our first love is something the first Church age was losing even while the Apostles walked the face of the earth.

How sad it is that we cannot comprehend in this age and every other, that to be born again of a new Spirit is only a seed, and only half of what makes us united in Christ as one with Him. The other half is to die to self, or to die to our lives even while in the body. Without one dying to His own life purposes and will, he cannot come alive in Christ and thereby mature the seed of the born again Spirit within him. When it is the only Spirit which moves his soul, perception of life, heart motives, and completely capturing the will, then one can say as Paul; it is no longer I who live, but Christ in me. The life you see me living is lived in faith in Jesus Christ who died in the body for me. Now Jesus lives His life in my body, and though alive in the body I am dead to my life, having no opportunity to give expression to it.

Notes

[14] Thorn, J. C. (n.d.). *Early Quaker History*. Retrieved October 2012, from John Countant Thorn's Home Page: http://thorn.pair.com/earlyq.htm

CHAPTER 10

Laodicea

The Seventh Church Age

To the Church in Laodicea

WEB Rev 3:14 *"To the angel of the assembly* (church) *in Laodicea write:*
"The Amen, the Faithful and True Witness, the Head of God's creation, says these things:
[15] "I know your works, that you are neither cold nor hot. I wish you were cold or hot. [16] So, because you are lukewarm, and neither hot nor cold, I will vomit you out of my mouth. [17] Because you say, 'I am rich, and have gotten riches, and have need of nothing;' and don't know that you are the wretched one, miserable, poor, blind, and naked; [18] I counsel you to buy from me gold refined by fire, that you may become rich; and white garments, that you may clothe yourself, and that the shame of your nakedness may not be revealed; and eye salve to anoint your eyes, that you may see. [19] As many as I love, I reprove and chasten. Be zealous therefore, and repent. [20] Behold, I stand at the door and knock. If anyone hears my voice and opens the door, then I will come in to him, and will dine with him, and he with me. [21] He who overcomes, I will give to him to sit down with me on my throne, as I also overcame, and sat down with my Father on his throne. [22] He who has an ear, let him hear what the Spirit says to the assemblies (churches).*"*

The seventh Church age is where we find ourselves today. This seventh Church age finds itself in the exact opposite standing as the sixth Church age. The sixth Church age had much going for them, and nothing against them. The seventh Church age has nothing going for them and much against them. However, it is important to take note that Jesus was not really addressing the *Church Corrupt* for a couple of ages now because they have become the seventh kingdom of Babylon. In the last couple of letters before this one, Jesus has been focused on affirming, admonishing, and encouraging what's left of the *Church Pure*, the "few." Likewise, in light of the seventh Church age, Jesus has already encouraged the *Church Pure* to hang on until

He returns. As such, He addresses the elect in the *Church Corrupt* in this final letter because the end has come. This explains why in the sixth Church age he found no fault when truly the *Church Corrupt* was flourishing during the same age. And in the seventh Church age Jesus found nothing redeeming, when truly there is a *Church Pure* because of what developed in the sixth Church age. The difference between the two ages are who Jesus is addressing.

It is here in the final letter to the seventh age of the Church that Jesus turns to and addresses the elect within the *Church Corrupt*. He continues to call individuals out of the corrupt Church system saying, right up to the very end I continue to stand at the door knocking. Then to the rest He tells them that they are so lost that they can't even see it about themselves. Time has run out and He has given every chance! He who walks among the lampstands speaks through time and tells the self-deluded and proud *Church Corrupt* that He is about to divorce them because of their unfaithfulness. They empower themselves with the spirit of this world, the spirit of the beast. Jesus does not say He is "about to" as in, "I am considering it." Rather, as in, "in just a few minutes I am going to." This seventh letter to the seventh Church age is not just a letter like the other six, but it is a certificate of divorce that Jesus is giving the *Church Corrupt*. This explains why after two letters of not addressing the *Church Corrupt*, He is finally speaking to them.

As a part of His divorce decree, Jesus gives advice on how to endure what the seventh Church age is about to suffer as a result of the divorce. He tells them this because it actually provides a final way out. If they show themselves true to their profession under the most terrible conditions, they will become the great multitude of celestial humans, taking part in the first resurrection.

The circumstances are as they were with Hosea and Gomer. After the adulteress Gomer prostitutes herself and has children with her lovers, Hosea buys her back at a price. She is hemmed in with tribulation. Through her tribulations she comes to her senses and realizes how she was better off with her husband. When Hosea takes her back it is only after a time of proven faithfulness before they restore their union. For that He vows his faithfulness to her. The great tribulation is that time of being hemmed in with troubles and the time to prove our profession faithful and true. Jesus had already paid the price for His bride.

What we received through Christ and the teachings of the Apostles has been affected and influenced by six major swings introduced into the Church. We live in a time that all of those influences throughout Church history have sway on our faith and the understanding of our salvation—our New Covenant relationship with Christ. The influences of these different ages (good or bad) have matured and worked their way throughout the entire Church Age; just as yeast does through a batch of dough. Everything is coming to its end.

Given all this: How, in these times, can we possibly know what to give ourselves over to? Which way is right? How is it possible to not be deceived? The answer is: It is not possible. However, Jesus agreeing, said:

Amp Mk 10:27 *Jesus glanced around at them and said, With men [it is] impossible, but not with God; for all things are possible with God.*

What we can learn from these seven letters is that it all comes down to the first letter. The only way to know is for the individual to regain Christ as his first love and it is only after that, it becomes the case as Jesus told us:

Amp Jn 7:17 *If any man desires to do His will (God's pleasure), he will know (have the needed illumination to recognize, and can tell for himself) whether the teaching is from God . . .*

The reformed church flocked to the open door of the Quakers which could not be closed. It facilitated the birth and formation of the United States, influencing its system of government which give personal freedom. However, when the perfection of finding what was lost from the beginning was revealed by the Quakers, the reformed church showed themselves as desirous of the blessings. However, and more importantly, they could not or would not fully return to their first love as the Quakers had.

The seventh Church age began around the time of the formation of this nation almost 250 years ago. Finally in 1776, a personal relationship with Jesus (religion) was separated from the worldly government which ruled this nation. This has not been the case since the Church gave itself over to Constantine's Roman Empire in 313 AD. The Church and the governments of this world had been one, but again in this nation the two were finally separated (church and state) as it was in the beginning. This was when the majority of the reformed church had realized the blessings of their strivings, but were unable to fully return to their first love (as demonstrated by the Quakers). Instead, they indulged themselves in the blessings that God gave. At that time the Church had risen to the ceiling above their heads. They were unable, even unwilling, to break through, as a result of being lovers of their own lives, and the freedom they created in forming this nation. They began to lust for personal independence and prosperity. This is what prevented them from fully returning to their first love.

The Seventh Church Age

For: None

Against/warning: *"I know your works, that you are neither cold nor hot. I wish you were cold or hot. Because you say, 'I am rich, and have gotten riches, and have need of nothing;' and don't know that you are the wretched one, miserable, poor, blind, and naked."*

What could be talking about the Church of this present age more than this, neither hot nor cold. He wishes we were one extreme or the other, and because we are not it is agonizing for Him. Ever been in a love relationship like this? This modern Church is richly blessed, especially in the west where its people primarily live in freedom of religion without government interference, with their needs met. They are committed to God but live for themselves. They profess to do His will, but where the rubber meets the road, they are only looking to get what they want out of life. They live for their own desires, spending their prayer life asking God to give them what they wish for.

Amp 2Ti 3:1 *BUT UNDERSTAND this, that in the last days will come (set in) perilous times of great stress and trouble [hard to deal with and hard to bear].*
Amp 2Ti 3:2 *For people will be lovers of self and [utterly] self-centered, lovers of money and aroused by an inordinate [greedy] desire for wealth, proud and arrogant and contemptuous boasters. They will be abusive (blasphemous, scoffing), disobedient to parents, ungrateful, unholy and profane.*
Amp 2Ti 3:3 *[They will be] without natural [human] affection (callous and inhuman), relentless (admitting of no truce or appeasement); [they will be] slanderers (false accusers,*

troublemakers), intemperate and loose in morals and conduct, uncontrolled and fierce, haters of good.

Amp 2Ti 3:4 [They will be] treacherous [betrayers], rash, [and] inflated with self-conceit. [They will be] lovers of sensual pleasures and vain amusements more than and rather than lovers of God.

Amp 2Ti 3:5 For [although] they hold a form of piety (true religion), they deny and reject and are strangers to the power of it [their conduct belies the genuineness of their profession].

As predicted, this church and its people are "lovers of themselves" having truly lost their first love. We have never (as a whole) returned to our first love (the error of the first Church age), with the exception of those starting with the sixth Church age who found what was lost. No, instead we have not returned and have made one error built upon another until we don't even understand that we are wretched, pitiful, poor, blind, and naked in spirit. Worthy of only divorce—to be spewed out of His mouth.

The Double-edged sword:

Words that give life: *"Be zealous therefore, and repent. Behold, I stand at the door and knock. If anyone hears my voice and opens the door, then I will come in to him, and will dine with him, and he with me. He who overcomes, I will give to him to sit down with me on my throne, as I also overcame, and sat down with my Father on his throne."*

As Jesus is about to give the *Church Corrupt* their certificate of divorce He beckons as many as will come out of her, the *Church Corrupt*, up to the last minute.

WEB Rev 3:18 I counsel you to buy from me gold refined by fire, that you may become rich; and white garments, that you may clothe yourself, and that the shame of your nakedness may not be revealed; and eye salve to anoint your eyes, that you may see. 19As many as I love, I reprove and chasten. Be zealous therefore, and repent.

This is the "counsel" Jesus is giving the elect in the *Church Corrupt*. He has just given a certificate of divorce to her because of unfaithfulness, "Buy gold refined in the fire." The gold is their reward which represents becoming celestial humans. The purifying fire that makes the gold is the great tribulation they are doomed to endure in either case. The garments of white are the celestial bodies they will attain if they stand on their testimony, do not worship the beast, or take his mark. Jesus then reminds them that He disciplines the ones He loves in hopes they will let it do the work in them which is needed. The only thing left is for the individuals to decide how they will endure the great tribulation they have been condemned to.

The words that give judgment: *"... because you are lukewarm, and neither hot nor cold, I will vomit you out of my mouth."*

This is the certificate of divorce Jesus gave the adulterous *Church Corrupt* taking His Spirit from them, leaving them to the time of the beast.

NIV Rev 3:3 Remember, therefore, what you have received and heard; obey it, and repent. But if you do not wake up, I will come like a thief, and you will not know at what time I will come to you.

Jesus had warned the fifth Church age when He released the prophetic voices who sparked the Reformation in the aftermath of the Black Plague during the fourth Church age. He had called the Church to "wake up" and return to what they had lost. He told them they were close to death and they needed to pull themselves up and pick up the pieces before it was too late. Only a portion of the Church got back to the basics. The rest did not heed His warning and now they have their certificate of divorce. Along with that divorce Jesus says that He will come like a thief and His church will be like the world, in that they will not know at what time He will come.

The first-century Christians understood very well what the end would look like. In Revelation, it says that the whole world, alive and dead, will be astonished, accept for those whose names are written in the Lambs book of life. The evidence which tells us the Church is in danger and has failed to repent and get back to first-century values is that in these days, the Church (as a whole) does not understand what will happen in the end. They have no clue how to interpret Daniel, the prophets, or the book of Revelation. However, all these things were well understood by the first-century Church.

This message, we the authors have released, is another grace from the Lord for: 1) In order that the *Church Pure* is not to be taken unaware, or uninformed. 2) To spark an end times revival which will: 1) Draw more of the elect out of her, the *Church Corrupt*, before it's too late. 2) To create no less than a civil war within the Church, giving the "enmity" needed to distinguish individuals between the seventh kingdom of the beast (the *Church Corrupt*) and the *Church Pure*. The *Church Pure* will be raptured and spared the suffering and destruction of the *Church Corrupt* (known to the Lord as Babylon). However, the endurance of that coming destruction is their last chance to be set free. That is, if their profession of faith remains true.

The characteristics of His person to this church: *"The Amen, the Faithful and True Witness, the Head of God's creation, says these things . . ."*

Jesus is saying, I tell the truth, this is the way it is going to happen; I am the final say and this is the final word/judgment!!!!!!! There is no wiggle room or reconsideration. This is the only way I can save you!

This is verified when He says, behold I will come like a thief! Again, He is saying this to the Church! We no longer have the inside scoop so we might be prepared. This is because clearly we are the object of His rebuke at this point. In the fifth Church age Jesus said, "If therefore you won't watch *(don't wake up)*, I will come as a thief, and you won't know what hour I will come upon you." Conversely, later in Revelation He says to His elect who had to endure the great tribulation:

NIV Rev 16:15 "Behold, I come like a thief! Blessed is he who stays awake . . ."

WEB Rev 13:9 If anyone has an ear, let him hear. 10 If anyone is to go into captivity, he will go into captivity. If anyone is to be killed with the sword, he must be killed.

It will take the great tribulation to purify His *Church Corrupt* and to separate her will from the pursuit of the things of this world. This is going to happen, these words are true. There is no fixing the Church. It will be vomited out of His mouth. It will not pay to attempt to fix the Church, unify the different churches/denominations, or work with the Church. This is the state of affairs of the Church. If it were not so, Jesus would not be saying it. Likewise, He is not saying that this is a "maybe" situation. He is saying this is what has and is becoming of the Church. It is how it will be when it comes time for the rapture and the great tribulation. This is why He has said to "come out of her all my saints so you don't suffer in her plagues."

So who is this message for, if this is the case and there is no hope of fixing this wretched condition? It is for the people, His people, His saints in the Church. It is time to stop being deluded, to stop tolerating that woman Jezebel—the woman who rides the beast. It is time to come out of her.

CHAPTER 11

Two Prophetic Dreams in Reference to the Seventh Church Age

Dream: The Ship Going Down

August 4, 2008

I was in this dark and old but very large house (The Church). There were 4 to 6 famous church leaders with me in this room. One was James McDonald. There was this guy I was having a hard time placing his face. Then I realized it was Dr. Robert Schuller. Everyone in the room was trying to convince me that there was something wrong with what I do and that I was not qualified. They were all dressed in pilgrim type outfits (the pilgrims and puritans represent those who almost got there but fell short of what the Quakers attained, and as a result persecuted the Quakers. Then they became stagnant in their pursuit of reformation, unable to grow further). When I finally recognized Dr. Robert Schuller, I said something and asked if it was him. He gave me a big smile and told me he wanted to show me something that might help me. He took me in this other room that was filled with books that he wrote. He told me pridefully that I should read them.

As he was trying to show me his books an emergency broke out. All the other leaders ran to help. But Robert wanted me to see all his books saying he would be there in a bit. I thought it strange that he would worry about that when our help was needed. I walked away politely. I came to the next room which was across an open area. Everyone was milling about in a panic. The church leaders were decisive and took action. There was this big flood of water (the end times).

I suddenly knew the big building was the Titanic and it was sinking (the Contemporary Church). This was weird because it was a house on land. But the water came and it was sinking. The Church leaders were running about organizing rescue and help. They were taking people one at a time through the water swimming them to safety. This would take too long and time was getting short. Besides, this place of safety was also going to be flooded soon. Because it was just another room in the same house that was sinking.

There were people in a panic and so self-absorbed that they lost their minds and could not do anything but panic, while taking up the time of others who had to tend to them. They had set up a triage area and were trying to get everyone out before it sunk in the water. However, once again they were just moving into another part of the same building. I didn't feel like I fit in. Nor did I see anything around me that was being done as productive. However, I was not afraid at all.

I wanted to help so I was trying to help this old fat woman by swimming her to safety (appealing to the Church at large with this message). However, she kept going back to get something and wanted too much explanation (the Church questioning our message but not acting on it, unwilling to give up what they have attained). She would start and then doubt. With my help she would make it to safety and then go right back, then start again, then stop. I realized I couldn't help many people that way (appealing to the Church by its leadership). The church leaders were very efficient, and organized but I somehow knew it was to no ends because it was like the blind leading the blind. They were noble, brave, and tireless. Their heroics were for nothing, because they could not stop what was happening or save anyone from it because they would not change their way of thinking. The dream was showing me that all of their polish and superficial but perfect integrity was wrong. It also showed that what I had been doing was right. Now that it mattered and was too late, the Church leaders had not opened their hearts to the true status of the Church.

Dream: It's Not Too Late!

March 2013

I dreamt that I stopped by my Dad's house and he was in his tomato garden. He didn't seem to want to talk to me and it was clear he had no respect for me or what I have to say. I pleaded with him to please give me just five minutes of his time. I told him that "I know you don't believe me now, but you will believe when I am not here anymore and have gone in the rapture." I was telling him of the things that would take place and warning him to not take the mark of the beast and that if he just holds true to his testimony of Jesus, even until death, that he will still make it to heaven. I explained to him the difference between the wheat and the grapes. It was really difficult for him to even take me seriously, but I was glad he let me say what I said, even if he was pretty dismissive so that when the time came, he would remember my plea and he would hopefully make the second cut (the first resurrection).

This dream was included because it perfectly represents what Jesus speaks to the seventh Church age at the end in Rev 3:18-21 in that He realizes there is no hope, they won't listen as what the dream concedes to:

"It was really difficult for him to even take me seriously, but I was glad he let me say what I said, even if he was pretty dismissive so that when the time came, he would remember my plea and he would hopefully make second cut."

What Jesus is saying to His Church is a kind of goodbye . . . I am about to divorce you and vomit you out of my mouth. This is my counsel, but it will be your choice because you will be on your own. What I had said to my Dad is what Jesus is saying to His Church in these verses, "please just give me five minutes of your time, I know you don't believe me now, but you will believe me when I am not here anymore." Remember my plea!

NIV Mt 23:12 For whoever exalts himself will be humbled, and whoever humbles himself will be exalted.
NIV Mt 23:13 "Woe to you, teachers of the law and Pharisees, you hypocrites! You shut the kingdom of heaven in men's faces. You yourselves do not enter, nor will you let those enter who are trying to.
NIV Mt 23:15 "Woe to you, teachers of the law and Pharisees, you hypocrites! You travel over land and sea to win a single convert, and when he becomes one, you make him twice as much a son of hell as you are.
NIV Mt 23:16 "Woe to you, blind guides! You say, 'If anyone swears by the temple, it means nothing; but if anyone swears by the gold of the temple, he is bound by his oath.'
NIV Mt 23:17 You blind fools! Which is greater: the gold, or the temple that makes the gold sacred?

NIV Mt 23:18 You also say, 'If anyone swears by the altar, it means nothing; but if anyone swears by the gift on it, he is bound by his oath.'

NIV Mt 23:19 You blind men! Which is greater: the gift, or the altar that makes the gift sacred?

NIV Mt 23:20 Therefore, he who swears by the altar swears by it and by everything on it.

NIV Mt 23:21 And he who swears by the temple swears by it and by the one who dwells in it.

NIV Mt 23:22 And he who swears by heaven swears by God's throne and by the one who sits on it.

NIV Mt 23:23 "Woe to you, teachers of the law and Pharisees, you hypocrites! You give a tenth of your spices—mint, dill and cummin. But you have neglected the more important matters of the law—justice, mercy and faithfulness. You should have practiced the latter, without neglecting the former.

NIV Mt 23:24 You blind guides! You strain out a gnat but swallow a camel.

NIV Mt 23:25 "Woe to you, teachers of the law and Pharisees, you hypocrites! You clean the outside of the cup and dish, but inside they are full of greed and self-indulgence.

NIV Mt 23:26 Blind Pharisee! First clean the inside of the cup and dish, and then the outside also will be clean.

NIV Mt 23:27 "Woe to you, teachers of the law and Pharisees, you hypocrites! You are like whitewashed tombs, which look beautiful on the outside but on the inside are full of dead men's bones and everything unclean.

NIV Mt 23:28 In the same way, on the outside you appear to people as righteous but on the inside you are full of hypocrisy and wickedness.

NIV Mt 23:29 "Woe to you, teachers of the law and Pharisees, you hypocrites! You build tombs for the prophets and decorate the graves of the righteous.

NIV Mt 23:30 And you say, 'If we had lived in the days of our forefathers, we would not have taken part with them in shedding the blood of the prophets.'

NIV Mt 23:31 So you testify against yourselves that you are the descendants of those who murdered the prophets.

NIV Mt 23:32 Fill up, then, the measure of the sin of your forefathers!

NIV Mt 23:33 "You snakes! You brood of vipers! How will you escape being condemned to hell?

NIV Mt 23:34 Therefore I am sending you prophets and wise men and teachers. Some of them you will kill and crucify; others you will flog in your synagogues and pursue from town to town.

NIV Mt 23:35 And so upon you will come all the righteous blood that has been shed on earth, from the blood of righteous Abel to the blood of Zechariah son of Berekiah, whom you murdered between the temple and the altar.

NIV Mt 23:36 I tell you the truth, all this will come upon this generation.

NIV Mt 23:37 "O Jerusalem, Jerusalem, you who kill the prophets and stone those sent to you, how often I have longed to gather your children together, as a hen gathers her chicks under her wings, but you were not willing.

NIV Mt 23:38 Look, your house is left to you desolate.

NIV Mt 23:39 For I tell you, you will not see me again until you say, 'Blessed is he who comes in the name of the Lord.'

Bibliography

American Standard Version. Scripture quotations marked (ASV) are taken from The American Standard Verion, which is in the public domain.

Amplified Bible. Scripture quotations marked (Amp) are taken from the Amplified Bible, Copyright © 1954, 1958, 1962, 1964, 1965, 1987 by The Lockman Foundation. Used by permission.

Antipas of Pergamum. (2013, March 6). Retrieved August 2013, from Wikipedia, The Free Encylopedia:
http://en.wikipedia.org/wiki/Antipas_of_Pergamum

Breathitt, B. L. (2007). 70 Ayin. Dream Symbols, 1(www.myonar.com). Breath of the Spirit Ministries.

Dankenbring, W. (n.d.). *Who are the "Nicolaitans".* Retrieved October 2012, from TriumphPro.com: www.triumphpro.com/nicolaitans.htm

Foxes' Book of Martyers: Chapter 2 The Ten Primitive Persecutions(n.d.). Retrieved November 2017, from Christian Classics Ethereal Library:
http://www.ccel.org/f/foxe/martyrs/fox102.htm

Joseph, G. N. (2008, December 25). *Biblical Numbers:1-10.* Retrieved October 2012, from Turnback to God: http://www.turnbacktogod.com/biblical-numbers-1-10/

Lolium temulentum. (2017, September 20). Retrieved December 2017, from Wikipedia, The Free Encylopedia:
https://en.wikipedia.org/wiki/Lolium_temulentum

New American Standard. Scripture quotations marked (NAS) are taken from the NEW AMERICAN STANDARD BIBLE®, Copyright © 1960,1962,1963,1968,1971,1972,1973,1975,1977,1995 by The Lockman Foundation. Used by permission.

New International Version. Scriptures taken from the Holy Bible, New International Version®, NIV®. Copyright © 1973, 1978, 1984 by Biblica, Inc.™ Used by permission of Zondervan. All rights reserved worldwide. www.zondervan.com The "NIV" and "New International Version" are trademarks registered in the United States Patent and Trademark Office by Biblica, Inc.™

New Living Translation. Holy Bible, New Living Translation copyright © 1996, 2004, 2007 by Tyndale House Foundation. Used by permission of Tyndale House Publishers Inc., Carol Stream, Illinois 60188. All rights reserved. New Living, NLT, and the New Living Translation logo are registered` trademarks of Tyndale House Publishers.

Nicolaism. (2014, January). Retrieved October 2012, from Wikipedia, The Free Encylopedia: http://en.wikipedia.org/wiki/Nicolaism

Parsons, J. J.(n.d.). *The Letter Ayin.* Retrieved October 2012, from Hebrew from Christians: http://www.hebrew4christians.com/Grammar/Unit_One/Aleph-Bet/Ayin/ayin.html

Pergamon. (2013, August 16). Retrieved August 2013, from Wikipedia, The Free Encyclopedia: http://en.wikipedia.org/wiki/Pergamon

Secret History of Papal Rome (n.d.). Retrieved December 2017, from End Times Prophecy: http://www.end-times-prophecy.org/secret-history-catholic-church.html

The Church at Smyrna. (n.d.). Retrieved October 2012, from Spiritjournals.com: http://www.spiritjournals.com/Special%20Sections/Persecuted%20Church/Articles/smyrna.htm

Thorn, J. C. (n.d.). *Early Quaker History.* Retrieved October 2012, from John Countant Thorn's Home Page: http://thorn.pair.com/earlyq.htm

Wein, B. a. (n.d.). *The Black Death.* Retrieved February 2014, from JewishHistory.org: http://www.jewishhistory.org/the-black-death/

World English Bible. Scripture quotations marked (WEB) are taken from The World English Bible, which is in the public domain. Specialthanks to Michael Paul Johnson and all who worked on the translation as a means to release a modern version of the Bible that is available for non-copyright use. A reminder that the Bible is not owned by man.

ABOUT THE AUTHORS

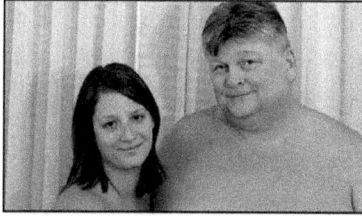

We are just a voice

WEB Jn 1:19 This is John's testimony (about himself), *when the Jews sent priests and Levites from Jerusalem to ask him, "Who are you?"*
WEB Jn 1:20 He declared, and didn't deny, but he declared, "I am not the Christ."
WEB Jn 1:21 They asked him, "What then? Are you Elijah?"
He said, "I am not."
"Are you the prophet?"
He answered, "No."
WEB Jn 1:22 They said therefore to him, "Who are you? Give us an answer to take back to those who sent us. What do you say about yourself?"
WEB Jn 1:23 He said, "__I am the voice__ of one crying in the wilderness, 'Make straight the way of the Lord ..."

True prophets in the Bible did not convince people who they were; in fact, they refused to talk about themselves. They refused to bring credibility to the words of God they spoke by trying to get people to believe who they were and trust them. They knew that it would be profaning the words of God to do so, and it would be elevating themselves above God's words. They knew that God's words have their own credibility because they are from God. And God will show them (His own words) as from Him.

God's prophets also knew that those who truly love God will, therefore, benefit from their words, and those who are lovers of themselves will not benefit from them, because they will be dismissive and not trust them. The time is over that we look at the person who speaks to decide if we believe. We must begin to discern if the words are from God and if they carry God's Spirit.

You might say to that, "but not everyone can discern God." If that is the case, then they indict themselves as not being "known" by Jesus. They unwittingly reveal about themselves that they desire to do their own will and not the Lord's, just as the religious leaders who wanted Jesus to prove His credibility so they could decide if His words were from God.

Amp Jn 7:16 *Jesus answered them by saying, My teaching is not My own, but His Who sent Me.* *Amp Jn 7:17* *If any man desires to do His will (God's pleasure), he will know (have the needed illumination to recognize, and can tell for himself) whether the teaching is from God or whether I am speaking from Myself and of My own accord and on My own authority.*

Many will think this is an oversimplified notion. However, it is so simple that it is not only true but reveals a simple but foundational truth about the person. What Jesus is saying is that if a man has a pure heart and wants to do the will of God above his own will, then what seems intuitively right (what sets well with that man) will be God's will and His words. However, even if you are a scholar, theologian, or work in the field of religion, and you desire to carry out your own will, having your own agendas and ambitions, well then, what seems right to that man is not God's will or His words, but that which lines up with his own will.

Generally speaking, the greatest religious minds in the world judge if something is from God by looking at the standing and qualifications of the man speaking them. In the above case, Jesus shows they may be smart in their own eyes, believing they know what is from God and therefore able to judge according to their knowledge of God. However, that would be saying in effect, we know everything about God because of our great knowledge. Therefore, if you say anything outside of our knowledge of God, or outside of the knowledge base of the accepted theological models, or if you are not a qualified student of those accepted models, then we must deduce your words are not from God.

To Jesus, they show about themselves that they don't recognize His words as from God because of their personal acquaintance with God. Instead, they have to judge by facts. They show themselves as having no real relationship with God; they would not recognize Him when He stands right before them. As a matter of fact, on another occasion when they showed contempt for Him, Jesus said of them:

NIV Jn 5:42 ... but I know you. I know that you do not have the love of God in your hearts.

They were once again wanting Him to prove who He was, and what right He had to talk the way He did. Jesus, instead of being intimidated, marveled at how He spoke and acted out everything the Father willed, yet they did not recognize His words as His Father's. Furthermore, they were, by nature, hostile and offended towards those words.

Let's look at that closer through an illustration. For example, you have a woman who claims to be married to a man named Jim. Then, a man claiming to be Jim and her husband approaches her. The above case is like the wife doubting this man is her husband. So then, she begins to question him. For example, "If you're Jim, when were you born?" And, "What kind of car did you have when you first got your license?" If he doesn't answer to her satisfaction, she decides that he is not her husband Jim. This might seem reasonable, and if he got the answers incorrect or didn't remember, the people listening might believe her when she says, "this is not my husband."

If there was anybody in the crowd that had wisdom, they might say this begs another question, "Hey lady, are you really Jim's wife or are you an imposter?" The reasoning of the wise man is, do you really need factual evidence to know if he is your husband? Don't you know your husband when he is standing right in front of you? Jesus is marveling at the religious leaders who are supposed to know God and claim to be in union with Him. However, they don't recognize Him when He stands before them. They don't even recognize His words as from God. Do they really need factual evidence to know something that they are supposed to have intimate knowledge of? Next question, why does it not occur to anyone to question if these men of God, leaders of the Jewish faith, may be imposters because they don't judge if someone and their words are from God by their intimate knowledge of God? They need factual evidence?

What did that tell Jesus? It told Him that even the top religious leaders who know the written word by heart can't recognize God when they stand right in front of Him.

It told Him that they were, in their inner man, hostile and threatened by God's words. It told Him that, in their inner selves, they really had no love or even any natural attraction towards God, His heart, and the Spirit of His words. They were obviously naturally repelled by them; they had no real love for God and their response showed it. However, to the religious leaders, they thought themselves wise and discerning to hold Jesus and His words suspect by judging Him with factual evidence. How disappointing it must have been to Jesus that the best of the best had no intimate knowledge of God and they were repulsed by Him when facing Him. Yes, Jesus' deduction was correct, there was no love of God in their hearts.

It is a Biblical fact that the major way we will be judged is it will be proven if we have a natural attraction to please God and do His will, therefore saying about us that we love Him more than ourselves. Learning by the folly of the leaders and the scholarly of Jesus' day, it is not by a knowledgeable and scholarly mind that one can successfully judge or discern what words coming from what person are from God or not. You can't judge superficially. No, it takes something much greater than to know every Bible verse by heart and to be able to have insightful knowledge of the person speaking them. It actually takes something much harder to attain than perfect scholarly knowledge of the written word. It takes a pure heart. Not meaning a sinless heart, but one which is single-minded, wanting to please God by serving Him and wanting to do His will at the expense of their own. This is what qualifies one to recognize if something is from God.

WEB Mt 5:8 *Blessed are the pure in heart, for they shall see God.*

It is true that as Colleen and I gain a larger following of our teachings and ministry, people will undoubtedly come to know us personally, and what kind of people we are. However, as teachers, we teach people how to live as spiritual men and women, discerning life in a spiritual way.

We have found the best way to teach discerning of spirit. It is not by knowing how to figure people out or to train them to have a spiritual power. No, we teach them to be single-minded when it comes to God, to be surrendered to His will in a pure or holistic way.

Having a still spirit which is not agitated with passions will create a huge contrast. The contrast of having the stillness of God's Spirit rule your heart coming in contact with the agitated spirit energies the people of this world operate out of makes one sensitive to discern spirit.

Jesus was right; wanting to do God's will with all your heart alone will cause you to recognize if one has God's Spirit in them and if they speak word's which are from God. As the saying goes, "You can't cheat an honest man."

NIV Jn 8:15 You judge by human standards. . .

NIV Jn 7:24 Stop judging by mere appearances, and make a right judgment."

As such, Colleen and I would like to be known first as a voice, just a voice. We want the words we speak from God to have more prominence and have their own credibility, than that of who we are. Therefore, we don't want to propagate people judging superficially if one is from God by giving our Bio. We want the words we speak to be more important than who we are. We want those who have a pure heart in wanting to serve God to check in their heart if we and the words we speak are from God.

We want those who don't have a pure heart to have a change of heart so they may know for themselves the voice and words of God when they hear them. However, we want to point people in the way to properly discern so they may know for themselves if we are from God and speak His words; in the same way John the Baptist tried to convey. You ask about us, and we will tell you about Him. You insist on wanting to know about us, and we will then tell you, we are just a voice making way for the One you should know and should be asking about. We are not a face or a name or people you should want to know, we are just a voice which gives voice to the One whose words you need to know.

OTHER BOOKS BY THE NAKED APOSTLES

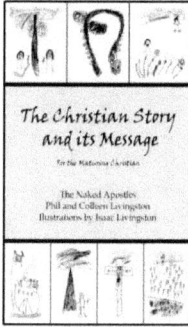

The Christian Story
and its Message

Christianity:
A Lost Civilization

For ordering information please visit our website at
www.nakedapostles.org

OTHER BOOKS BY THE NAKED APOSTLES

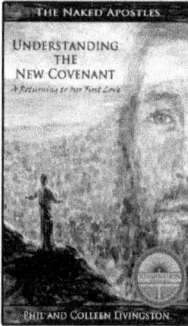

Understanding
the
New Covenant:
*A Returning to Our
First Love*

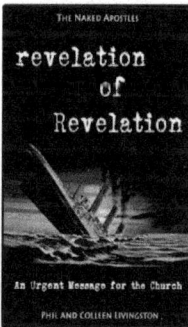

revelation of Revelation:
*An Urgent Message
for the Church*

Volumes 1-6

For ordering information please visit our website at
www.nakedapostles.org